A TIME TO SPEAK

The Selected Prose of
ARCHIBALD
MacLEISH

A
TIME
TO
SPEAK

The Selected Prose of
ARCHIBALD
MᴀᴄLEISH

MCMXLI

Houghton Mifflin Company, Boston · The Riverside Press, Cambridge

The Riverside Press
CAMBRIDGE · MASSACHUSETTS
PRINTED IN THE U.S.A.

ACKNOWLEDGMENTS

GRATEFUL acknowledgment is made to the following magazines and publishers.

To *The Atlantic Monthly* for 'Poetry and the Public World' and 'Of the Librarian's Profession'; to *The Yale Review* for 'Public Speech and Private Speech in Poetry'; to *Poetry Magazine* for 'In Challenge, not Defense' and 'Nevertheless One Debt'; to the *Saturday Review of Literature* for 'An Anonymous Generation,' and 'The Poetry of Karl Marx'; to *The Forum* for 'Preface to an American Manifesto'; to *The New Masses* for 'Mr. Sandburg and the Doctrinaires' and 'The Communists, The Writers, and the Spanish War'; to *Stage* for 'A Stage for Poetry'; to *New Theatre* for 'Question of Audience'; to *Life* for 'Portrait of a Living Man'; to *Survey Graphic* for 'The Affirmation,' and 'Freedom to End Freedom'; to *The Nation* for 'The Art of the Good Neighbor'; to Duell, Sloan and Pearce, Inc. for 'The Irresponsibles,' and to *Fortune* for the following selections: 'Death of an Era' from 'Ivar Kreuger I,' 'Green River' from 'Grasslands,' 'Landscape of a People' from 'Japan,' 'Of Many Men on Little Land' from 'Japan,' 'Argentina of the Plate: Argentina of the Pampas' from 'Argentina,' and 'Postcards and Haciendas' from 'Chile.'

CONTENTS

IN CHALLENGE, NOT DEFENSE

THE time is past for the defenses of poetry. The defenses have all been written. The time now is for the challenges.

The patient, kidding, ironical challenges to those who tell us poetry is dead. Let them bury it then. Let them bury the big bones of Yeats and the Hamlet-grinning skull of Eliot and the man-smelling shirt of Carl Sandburg and the splintered china and bright glass of Wallace Stevens and the quiet cricket-talking of Frost in the dead leaves and the mole-rummaging under the lot of Ezra Pound and the tens and twenties of young ones writing a great line like a motto cut into marble and throwing it out like trash for the promise of something better just beyond. Let them bury them all if they can, heaping the disappointed, middle-ageing words on the top for an epitaph. Let them bury them all and go off with the crocodile tears in their eyes and return with the next day's sun to the big hole in the ground and the snicker of grasshoppers.

The loud-mouthed, disrespectful, horse-laughing challenges to those who tell us poetry is 'pure.' Those who tell us poetry is 'poetry.' Those who tell us poetry is a parlor game and has no truck with the living of live men or the misery of hungry men or the politics of ambitious men or the indignation of believing men. Those who tell us the eternal poetry is the poetry written about the feeling of

1

being dreadfully alone. Those with the High Standards. (The impotent have the High Standards: the begetters beget.) Those with the Love of Posterity. (Posterity is the offspring of the childless.) Those who escape into mirrors — into the gentleman-farms and the upstairs rooms with the view of the river and the seminars at five P.M. The loud-mouthed disrespectful challenge to all such to come out of their words and their paragraphs into the open air of the art and say their say in the sun with the wind blowing. The loud-mouthed disrespectful challenge to look at the actual world and say what poetry is native to the actual world: to read the poetry of Dante and say what poetry is native to the actual world; to read the poetry of Shakespeare and say what poetry is native to the actual world; to lay their High Standards down alongside the poetry of Dante and of Shakespeare and see how small an inch their yardstick measures in the actual world.

The time is past for the defenses and the time has come for the challenges because there is no way of stating the defense of poetry which does not become a challenge. There is no way of asking whether we should permit poetry to continue to exist which does not ask instead whether poetry will permit us to continue to exist. For it is the second question and not the first which is sensible and which must be answered. The first is a question for the debating societies in the preparatory schools. The second is a question for mortal men.

We live in a time of crisis in which the heart of the crisis is that question. The crisis of our time, as we are beginning slowly and painfully to perceive, is a crisis not of the hands but of the heart. It is a crisis of hunger — but not a crisis of hunger created by any doubt as to our ability to feed ourselves. It is a crisis of cold — but not a crisis of

cold created by any doubt as to our ability to put roofs
over our heads or clothes on our backs. It is a material
crisis in which there is not now, nor has there ever been
since the beginning of these times, the least question of our
material wealth. It is a crisis, in other words, of which the
entire cause lies in the hearts of men.

The failure is a failure of desire. It is because we the
people do not wish — because we the people do not know
what it is that we should wish — because we the people do
not know what kind of world we should imagine, that this
trouble hunts us. The failure is a failure of the spirit: a
failure of the spirit to imagine; a failure of the spirit to
imagine and desire. Human malevolence may perhaps
have played its part. There are malevolent men as there
are stupid men and greedy men. But they are few against
the masses of the people and their malevolence, like their
stupidity, could easily be swept aside if the people wished:
if the people knew their wish.

Last year and the year before that and the year before
that year men used to talk of the paradox of starvation in
the midst of plenty. The implication was that we starved
because there were evil men who wished that we should
starve or incompetent men who were unable to provide us
with food. But truly it was not at all this that the paradox
of starvation in the midst of plenty implied. The true implication of the bread lines under the heaped-up wheat
elevators in Minneapolis was the failure of the people, of
ourselves the people, to imagine the world in which we
wished to believe.

For once we had imagined that world we had only to
reach out our hands to make it real. Never before in the
history of this earth has it been more nearly possible for a
society of men to create the world in which they wished to

live. In the past we assumed that the desires of men were easy to discover and that it was only the means to their satisfaction which were difficult. Now we perceive that it is the act of the spirit which is difficult: that the hands can work as we wish them to. It is the act of the spirit which fails in us. With no means, or with very few, men who could imagine a common good have created great civilizations. With every means, with every wealth, men who are incapable of imagining a common good create now ruin.

This failure of the spirit is a failure from which only poetry can deliver us. In this incapacity of the people to imagine, this impotence of the people to imagine and believe, only poetry can be of service. For only poetry, of all those proud and clumsy instruments by which men explore this planet and themselves, *creates the thing it sees*. Only poetry, exploring the spirit of man, is capable of creating in a breathful of words the common good men have become incapable of imagining for themselves. Only poetry, moving among living men on the living earth, is capable of discovering that common world to which the minds of men do, inwardly, not knowing it, assent.

Certainly the economists to whom we have thus far appealed in the disasters of our time cannot help us. Mathematicians of the mob, their function is to tell us what, as mob, we *have* done. When they call their observations laws and bridge the future with them, all their work falls down. When they try to build their theories out beyond the past, ahead of history, they build like wasps with paper. And for this reason — their laws come after, not before, the act of human wishing: and the human wish can alter all they know. In Germany and Italy where men, some men, enough men to have power, have imagined lifelike melodramas to take up the lack of life, the world's economists are made to look like infants. Both states by every economic rule have been insolvent now for years. And yet they arm, build planes, wage wars, kill Spanish women the economists would say they could not build nor wage nor kill. Economists, like all historians, believe the future from the past. The future differs from the past in one particular: men wait for it and men can change. Men can grow tired and discouraged and wish change. Men can grow tired of the old excuses and the threadbare frauds and wish new answers. The man who gives them answers from the past and says: 'You did this once; you'll do this twice,' will not persuade them when they're truly tired.

Only poetry that waits as men wait for the future can persuade them. The Church cannot. The Church concerns itself with souls, but with each soul alone and for a different purpose. It possesses an eternal truth in which the ages of the human spirit, the great successive images which one by one have moved the hearts of men, are like the little winds that blur the sea. It solves the difficult arithmetic of this hard world by writing the equations on a blackboard somewhere else. Poetry can have no elsewhere. Poetry is art and, being art, committed to this earth, confined within the shallow water of this air. Its matter is what men can see and sense and know. Its medium is speech: most common, human, touched, and worn of all materials that men have used for art. Its end is man: not men alone, not men in secret — men as they are different — men turned souls and grown distinguishable for eternity, but man. The common loveliness that all men everywhere have known: the common fears: the common passions: the despairs.

Why do poets, generation after generation, time out of mind, repeat: The sea is beautiful; women are beautiful;

the sun is beautiful? Because for each man it is new? No.
Because for all men it is old. Because the loveliness, the
poetry, is in the commonness, the recognition. Because it
is the love, the wonder, that is poetry and not the object
of the love or wonder. Generation after generation poetry
has kept this record of the hearts of men. We who are now
alive, the poets say, we men now living in this earth, we
are still loyal to the sun: we are still loyal to the evening
and the odor of the water in the evening.

Poetry alone in such a time as ours when all the images
are blurred and doubtful, when men go starved because
they cannot wish in common — poetry alone imagines, and
imagining creates, the loyalty for lack of which we cannot
live; for lack of which we cannot even eat, be covered and
be warm. Poetry alone imagines, and imagining creates,
the world that men can wish to live in and make true. For
what is lacking in the crisis of our time is only this: this
image. Its absence *is* the crisis. The issues men call issues
are no issues. The issue between a planned economy and
an economy called free is not an issue. The issue between a
big-unit regulated economy and a small-unit competitive
economy is not an issue. Such differences are differences of
tactics, differences of means. The fact that we can talk of
them as though they touched the life and death of our
society merely betrays the poverty of our minds. Actually
the issue, the one issue, we should talk about is this: What
do we love? What truly do we love? To what do we desire
to be loyal? Once we know the answer to that question,
everything will follow of itself. Once we know the thing
that we desire to be, the things that we must do will follow
of themselves.

The defense of poetry in this time is a challenge. It is a

challenge to all those who quarrel about the means by which the people shall be saved to hold their tongues and be silent until the poets shall have given the people speech. It is a challenge to all those who would stop the mouths of the poets with their pantry notions of pure poetry and their gentleman's gentleman's Standards of what a poet does, to hold their tongues and be humble until the poets have been heard. A poet, like any other artist, like any other honest man acting as an honest man, does what he must do, what he has no choice but do. In a time like ours his poetry is like the poetry written in this time, for he has no choice but write such poetry. He writes *the people yes* because the *yes* of the people boils up through all the lovely images of the lake beyond the dunes, and all the glimpses backward into personal time, and will not let him rest until it is written. And writing it he brings the mind of this nation one step nearer to an understanding of its will, and one step nearer to an imagination of the world in which it can believe and which, believing, it can bring about.

Those who wish authority for such conclusions may have authority. The authority is Aristotle's. In that great unfinished definition of poetry in which Aristotle distinguished poetry from history he said: history draws things which have happened but poetry things which may possibly happen. In that word 'possibly' is the whole aesthetic to justify the human and world-walking poetry of this generation. For the possibility of which Aristotle speaks is human possibility. History draws things which have happened: poetry things which are possible to men. In this time in which everything is possible except the spirit to desire and the love to choose, poetry becomes again the one deliverer of the people.

July, 1938.

THE AFFIRMATION

I T IS the nature of liberalism to ask questions and not to answer them. The question which American liberalism asks itself in this time, however, is a question which must be answered. For American liberalism, which has been a disinterested and judicial observer of so many conflicts in so many parts of the world, remote and near, now finds itself an observer of a conflict in which it can be neither disinterested nor judicial because that conflict involves itself, and threatens its own right to exist. If the mutiny against moral law, the treason against intellectual truth, which we call fascism destroys democratic society, it will destroy liberalism as well. Liberalism, therefore, is a party to the struggle. And the question is simply this: What does American liberalism propose to do about it? How does American liberalism propose to defend democratic society against the treason of fascism? What policy of defense does American liberalism believe should be adopted?

The issue can be stated more narrowly and more specifically. Logically, and practically as well, there are two broad alternatives. An attempt can be made to defend democracy against fascism by adopting an *anti*-fascist policy, or an attempt can be made to defend democracy against fascism by adopting a *pro*-democratic policy. The first is the policy adopted by the Communist Party.[1] It is a defensive policy which devotes its efforts and its means altogether to the weakening of fascism by the exploitation of fascism's cruelties, stupidities and defects. The second is the policy so far adopted by no one. In theory it would be an affirmative and offensive policy which would devote its efforts and the means at its disposal to the strengthening of democracy. The question which American liberalism must answer is whether it will follow the Communist Party into a policy of anti-fascism or whether it will adopt the alternative policy of aggressive pro-democratic action aimed, not at the exploitation of the weakness of fascism, but at the realization of the potential strength of democracy. To my way of thinking the answer to this question will almost certainly determine the future form of American society. It is an answer which must be given very soon.

There is a great deal to be said — or rather a great deal *is* said — for the first, the anti-fascist, alternative. It is said that anti-fascism is the only realistic policy because only on the negative line of anti-fascism is it possible to form a common front of all opinions, and only by a common front of all opinions is it possible for democracy to win. It is said that anti-fascism is the only sound psychological policy, since the love of democracy is itself a negative thing, being no more than the hatred of tyranny, and since the hatred of fascism supplies again the hatred of tyranny which is necessary to give the love of democracy vitality and force. It is said, in short, that anti-fascism, both practically and ideally, is the policy which should be adopted.

Speaking alone for myself I must dissent from these arguments and their conclusion. I do not believe that anti-

[1] Written prior to the Berlin-Moscow Pact.

9

fascism is the only realistic policy of defense. And the reason I disbelieve it is precisely the reason advanced in its support. It is undoubtedly true that only on the negative line of anti-fascism is it possible to form a common front of all opinions in defense of democracy. But the reason why it is possible to form a common front of all opinions on the negative line of anti-fascism is precisely that it is *not* democracy which is being defended on that line but the status quo. It is the defense of the status quo which brings together the Chicago *Tribune* and Mr. Ickes and the State Department and the C.I.O. and the D.A.R. and the radio announcers and the people who pay income taxes and the people who do not pay income taxes. And the policy which proposes to fight fascism by defending the status quo is not a realistic policy, but an extremely unrealistic policy because the status quo *cannot be defended.* A status quo of which the most noticeable characteristic is ten millions of unemployed cannot be defended against fascism. The frontiers of the status quo can be fortified, and should be fortified, against attacks from abroad. But fascism, as we have seen in Spain, as we have seen in Czechoslovakia, as we have seen here also, does not attack from abroad. It attacks in the back rooms, in the dark of the railroad trestles, in the sand-lots down by the river, in the loudspeaker on the kitchen table where the grating voice of the ambitious priest rattles the pitiful dishes with spite and hate. It attacks where the fleets and the coast-defense guns and the bombers of the status quo cannot intercept it. It attacks where the status quo is vulnerable — within. The common front which can be formed to defend the status quo against fascism is a common front which stands with its back to the real danger.

It is time, it seems to me, for American liberalism to recognize the real danger for what it is and to call it by its proper name. The communist leadership against fascism, which liberals generally follow, is unable, for obvious reasons, to face the fascist facts. It is, understandably, committed to the theory that fascism is the seizure of power by a decaying capitalism to forestall the seizure of power by the protelariat. That theory does not fit the history of Germany and Italy nor does it fit the probabilities of the situation here. On the contrary it produces just such errors of liberal judgment as the policy of the common front for the defense of the status quo. If fascism is the coup d'état of a frightened and desperate capitalism, then one way to prevent fascism is to reassure the capitalists by promising to respect the status quo, and another and even better way to prevent fascism is to line up side by side with the capitalists for the defense of the status quo against armed attack from outside. But fascism is not the coup d'état of a frightened and desperate capitalism. Fascism is the coup d'état of a class which is as hostile to the ruling-class capitalists as it is to the proletariat of Marx: a class which denies the right of the capitalists to govern as vigorously as it denies the right of the proletariat of Marx to inherit: a class which claims that it, and not the proletariat of Marx, will take over from the dying capitalists, and that it will take over not in the interest of these dying capitalists but of itself.

This class is the class which in all modern, industrialized societies is potentially the most dangerous because it is the most ignorant, the most violent, the most brutal and the most unhappy. It is the class which the Industrial Revolution and the capitalist money system produced between them — the class which the Industrial Revolution, with its

11

need for specialized labor and its liberal theories of education, pulled up and away from the masses who labor with their hands — the class which the capitalist money system, with its limited opportunities and its materialistic values, left hanging just above brute labor, just below comfort and decency and self-respect. Fascism in Italy and in Germany was the successful revolt of this class. Fascist parties in other countries are parties of this class. The reason why fascism is so brutal, so vulgar, so envious, so ignorant, so superstitious, so childish, so shrewd, so dishonest, is that these are the characteristics, not of a single dictator acting for some hidden clique of terrified financial magnates or other mysterious persons, but of this class. Capitalism is responsible for this fascist class. Capitalism created it and consigned it to live in the limbo between the worlds, seducing it from the discipline of hand labor on the one side, denying it the discipline of head labor on the other; depriving it, on the one side, of the realism, the hard-headedness, the piety, the traditional human wisdom, the salt sense, the kindness of those who labor the earth, and the earth's trees and the earth's metals, with their hands; depriving it, on the other, of that different kindness, that different knowledge, that different faith of those whose life is in the mind. But though capitalism created the fascist class, capitalism can neither control it now nor use it. Fascism is capitalism's revenge upon itself: an old and dying king eaten by the children his own crimes conceived.

Clearly then the allegedly realistic policy of defense against fascism which proposes to fortify the frontiers of the status quo is not a realistic policy of defense against the actual fascist danger, for it is the status quo which has created this actual fascist danger. The only possible defense against the treason of the fascist class is the strength-

ening of democratic institutions and democratic loyalty
within the country. A nation moving radically and vigorously toward a believable democratic objective is not a
nation in which a fascist coup d'état is possible. A nation
standing still and defending a static and decadent economy
is a nation in which a fascist coup is all but inevitable.

But if anti-fascism, as a realistic policy, is indefensible,
so too is the rationalization of that policy which argues
that anti-fascism will reinvigorate democracy — that it
will supply again the hatred of tyranny and the fear of op-
pression upon which the love of democracy rests. It is
undoubtedly true that the love of liberty involves the
hatred of despotism. But there is a difference between *inventing* liberty out of hatred for despotism, and *defending*
liberty against the fear of despotism. The hatred of tyranny which results in the invention of liberty is one thing:
it produces a new and affirmative act of belief and hope.
The fear of tyranny which accompanies the defense of a
liberty already won is another: it remains only fear. And a
policy which rests upon fear is a dangerous policy to depend
upon because fear is a short-winded emotion.

People get over indignation. They get over horror. They
even get over fear. What they don't want to remember
drains easily from their minds. Darwin noted long ago
that observations and thoughts contrary to his conclusions
disappeared from his mind more readily than observations
and thoughts which were favorable to his conclusions.
We too have seen how easily things we wish we didn't know
escape from our memories. We have seen newsreel pictures
taken in Spain and China which were unforgettable. We
have forgotten them. We suffer now the bitter indignation
which only cold-blooded cruelty such as Franco's can in-
spire. And we will forget that indignation. Indeed we will

forget this last and angriest indignation sooner than the others, for people forget the shocking and the shameful and the terrible the more readily as it is the more shocking and the more shameful. For a generation after the Civil War people debated Sherman's responsibility for the burning of half of Atlanta — a fire in which no one died. A few months after the Nazi bombing of Guernica and the fascist slaughter in the bull-ring at Badajoz, we have forgotten both Guernica and Badajoz.

Speaking still for myself I can only say that I do not believe in the negative policy, the defensive policy, the anti-fascist policy. I believe only in an affirmative policy, an offensive policy, a pro-democratic policy. I believe that American liberalism must refuse to follow the communist lead, that it must refuse to forego its own nature and its own purposes, that it must refuse to identify democracy with the status quo, that it must become not less liberal, less radical, but more liberal, more radical. I believe that American liberalism must become more liberal, not less liberal, as the danger in Europe becomes more acute. I believe that American democracy must invent and continually reinvent its democracy; that it must attack, not defend.

Briefly, I believe that American liberalism must accept the full obligation of its decision to defend democracy against fascism. It must ask itself: 'What do we mean by democracy?' And it must answer that question. It must answer: 'We mean by democracy a society in which the dignity of man is of first importance, a society in which everything else must be subject to, and must support, the dignity of man.' In Marxist theory economics comes first — all politics is economics and economic necessity determines political action. In fascist practice, politics comes

14

first — all economics is politics and the political police determine the operation of economic laws. In democratic theory man comes first — both politics and economics are subjected to the advancement of the dignity and decency of man.

What our American liberalism must do in this crisis, and in this crisis more than at any other time, is to apply the definition of democracy to the times and to say how and by what means democracy in these times can be strengthened and made vigorous.

More precisely and more practically, what American liberalism must do in this crisis is to forego the characteristic liberal attitude of critical correction and accept instead the risks of action.

It must put aside the irresponsible self-righteousness with which it sometimes judges the decisions of those charged with the government of the republic and accept instead its share of responsibility for that government.

It must accept responsibility for steps already taken which lead in the direction a dynamic democracy should go — steps like the Tennessee Valley Authority, the Federal Arts Projects, the techniques developed by the Department of Agriculture for the democratic control of programs of production — and exert its strength to extend those experiments in their own fields and to invent their analogues elsewhere.

An American writer who has seen more of our time than most of us have seen, remarks that there are two minds in the world. There are those who believe in getting things done. And there are those who believe in being right. The distinction is notorious enough in the Marxist movement where those who believe in being right have acquired a name and an unenviable reputation of their own. But there are Trotskyists elsewhere and not least among liberals. There are liberals who enjoy the sterile and rancid pleasures of self-righteousness, liberals who prefer the safety of a spinsterish and impotent intellectualism to the risks of affirmation and belief. It is these liberals who have given to American liberalism its characteristic tone of moral self-satisfaction, intellectual snobbishness, and inability to act. If they continue to direct liberal thinking in this country, shaming into silence and inaction those who believe that in liberalism also action is important and ends must be achieved, American liberalism will remain what it is and the questions it must ask itself will go unanswered.

But if American liberalism will shake off that impotent and dilettante control, and face the fact that it also is a party to these wars, it may perhaps exert a controlling influence on their outcome. At least it may supply a direction and a program which American democracy now lacks.

May, 1939.

PREFACE TO AN AMERICAN
MANIFESTO

N O MAN really concerned with the failure of the
revolutionary movement in America need de-
ceive himself as to the cause. The cause is
obvious. The American revolutionary move-
ment has stalled because it is a movement conceived, delivered, and nurtured in negatives. Its impulse is hatred.
Its one convincing aim is the destruction of the existing
order. Its one vital dream is the establishment of a repressive control which will make the destruction of the existing
order permanent and complete. And its leaders, the writers and journalists who shape its thought, are for the most
part intellectual terrorists, seizing whatever concept will
most effectively destroy. There are, of course, great and
notable exceptions. There are men like John Dos Passos
who are moved by a generous passion for justice profound
as the instinct of an animal. But for the most part the
emotion which excites and inspires American revolutionary
writers is the emotion of hate.

And from hatred there springs no life. Not even when
its object is worthy of its spleen. The Great American
Capitalist and his son and his daughter-in-law and his
banking system might well have been begotten explicitly
for hatefulness. They have all the attributes of hateful-

ness: they are greedy; they are arrogant; they are gross;
they lack honor; their existence insults the intelligence.
It is a pleasure — almost a duty — to hate them. But
the emotion with which they are regarded is hatred nevertheless. And hatred merely kills. To crucify a banker in
the name of the brotherhood of man is to crucify a banker
and no more. Unless it serve to justify Carl Sandburg's
pungent saying that the brotherhood of man 'is sometimes
not so much a beautiful dream as a humiliating reality.'

The great vice of hatred, the reason why moralists have
condemned it, is that it brings about, not the creation of
new life, but merely the destruction of old. The man who
carries his loathing tied around his neck like a dead bird
has but one notion of heaven — to be rid of the rotting
thing. And to be rid of evil is not to obtain good. Revolutions which are made merely *against* the existing world are
inevitably made in its opposite — which is to say in its
image. And revolutionary thinking of the so-called realistic and scientific kind which develops the future inevitably,
and by inescapable evolution, out of the ills of the present
and the evils of the past is revolutionary thinking in which
all the virtues of tomorrow are merely the absence of the
vices of today. It is a wonderful thing for men living under
exploitation to look forward to the day when they shall no
longer live under exploitation. But it is also a wonderful
thing for a man living under the agony of a wound to look
forward to the day when the agony of the wound shall be
gone. And nevertheless absence of pain, as almost all men
have learned who have experienced it, is not at all the
same thing as the presence of pleasure.

It is for this reason that so much of the revolutionary
writing of our time is flat. Or rather it is for this reason
that so much of it sounds flat in the crisis of the spirit in

which we find ourselves. In casual times there is a considerable excitement and satisfaction to be taken from the magazine articles and the books and the editorials which let fly at the plate-glass windows of the world with anything which may have weight enough to break them. But in years such as these men require something else. They require a believable purpose in destruction. They require a believable picture of something better to come. And when they are given instead a kind of intellectual misrepresentation and fraud — when the promises implied in a writer's indictment of the existing world are never, in his prophecies of a better world, performed — the result is a sense of flatness and disillusion and defeat. The preamble, the instigation to revolt, may be as persuasive as it pleases. The Whereas-es may explode like trench bombs. The detonations may be superb. Capitalism may hang in tatters of bloody meat along the wire. But if the rest is rubbish, if the Therefores, the conclusions, march in upon the conquered field like the four Fratellinis introduced by a ten-day bombardment, the net result will be disappointing. And if the world is informed that this disappointment is the glorious victory for which the wars are all to be fought, the sentiment of disappointment may be sharpened to disgust. It is not enough to tell a man that, after so much suffering and so many years, he may at last, and as the ultimate reward, set up a small, blank tombstone burying the past.

But the most curious effects of this passion for the negative are to be seen, not among revolutionary writings, but among revolutionary writers. Nowhere in our time is it possible to discover a more devious self-contradiction and defeat than among the intellectuals of the Left. Men whose personal inclinations, whose artistic necessities, lead them

19

to desire the greatest bodily and spiritual freedom use their
entire influence and all the power of their art to advance
an order under which neither bodily nor spiritual freedom
can exist — their sole reason being that only such an order
can terminate the practices of men whom they detest.
But to act in opposition to one's enemy is not to act as a
free man. And to replace Mr. Insull merely by that which
will make Mr. Insull's return impossible is to grant Mr.
Insull the greatest privilege one generation can bestow
upon another — the kingly privilege of fixing the succes-
sion to the throne. If only an iron tombstone will keep Mr.
Insull from rising, then it is Mr. Insull who has designed
the iron tombstone.

What is necessary to the free man, what is above all
necessary to the free writer, is to consider *without reference
to his enemies* the kind of world he himself would like to
bring about. That world for all artists, for all men of
spirit is the democratic world, the world in which a man
is free to do his own work, the world in which a man may
think as he pleases, the world in which a man may, with
the complete responsibility of a mature individual, control his proper life. There are only two objections to the
democratic world. One is that it has been destroyed by
the practices of capitalism. The other is that it is difficult
of realization in an industrial society. Both in essence
come down to the same thing: that the re-establishment of
democracy in modern America would be a very difficult
thing.

As to that there is one point to be made at the outset.
Democracy has always been difficult of realization. It is
the most difficult of all known forms of government to
administer. It was difficult in 1787. It was the opinion
of Hamilton that it was impossibly difficult. But the rea-

son why it is difficult is precisely that it is designed, not in the interest of economic efficiency or political expediency, but in the interest of the richest and freest human life. It is therefore at a disadvantage in comparison with all forms of autocratic government designed solely in the interest of efficiency — forms of government which either ignore altogether the problem of a decent and human life for the members of society or postpone its consideration to some unnamed future day when, after the sacrifice of many generations to tyranny, the good life is assumed to follow in some mysterious way of its own volition. But such disadvantage is a challenge, not an obstacle. And particularly is it a challenge to the artist.

There are, it is true, a certain number of artists who do not desire freedom and responsibility; who do not wish to be remitted to their own lives, naked against an unknown universe; who long, instead, for a social womb to which they may return and where safely they may lie while the blood of a social organism is pumped through their hearts in substitution for their own blood, and the thoughts of a social mind are dreamed through their brains in substitution for their own thoughts. These are the men who announce that the old vitality is dead, and that the new art will be the mass expression of a conglomerate mind. They are the spiritual infants whose sole longing is to cuddle back into the anonymous and undemanding dark. For the rest, for the adult, for those who accept the responsibilities of their lives, the fact that democracy is the most difficult of governments is the highest of commendations — the greatest praise.

They will ask only one question — whether the difficulties are so great as to be insurmountable. The contention usually made is that democracy is an expression of individualism, that the industrial age is collectivist, and that democracy is therefore finished. But if these cant terms are translated back into the English language, it will be discovered that what is meant is merely this: that democracy was all right in a world in which people lived separate lives, and in which the sole function of government was to keep them from breaking into each other's houses; but that democracy is all wrong in a world in which people are drawn by the efficiency of their machines into a life so complicated that the function of government must be to control almost everything. Now the answer to that contention is very simple indeed. It is one word: 'Why?' Political democracy, the kind of democracy of which we keep the empty shell today, may be incompetent to run an industrial society. But who contends that the political democracy embalmed by the Republican Party since the Civil War is democracy? The individualism of the Empire Builders, the kind of individualism which is all rights and no duties, may be incompatible with governmental control of industry. But who contends that the individualism of the Empire Builders is the individualism of the democratic ideal? There is, as a matter of fact, considerable proof that that kind of individualism, the kind of individualism around which the conservatives now wrap the sacred garment of the Constitution, was unknown to constitutional law before 1865.

True democracy is a form of government in which the control of society lies eventually in the hands of all its members. It is, in theory, as wholly applicable to the control of industry as to the control of those political fields in which it has traditionally operated. All that is necessary is to find a technique of control. And such techniques, difficult though they may be, have already been suggested — the most important doubtless being techniques for the democratic control of credit. If they can be worked out to practical demonstration, then it will be clear that the difficulties of applying democratic control to an industrial society are not insurmountable.

The whole question to my mind comes down to this: Shall we in America be driven by our hatred of the existing system or drawn by our hopes for the new? Shall we move directly toward the best kind of life we can conceive, even though the means be difficult, or shall we take the easier and brutal short cut to an efficient control of industrial society by dictatorship — hoping eventually for that far, far distant, classless society which Karl Marx permitted his congregations to glimpse over the million heads of many sacrificed and immolated generations — that classless society which retreats as rapidly as communism with *its* privileged class advances?

To talk of 'the best kind of life' is to invite the charge of Utopianism. And I accept the charge. There is no possible substitute for Utopian thinking. Certain admirers of the great founder of modern socialism remark with enthusiasm that his contribution to that theory was to make scientific and precise what had before been ideal and visionary. It is a characteristic nineteenth-century commendation, and one which carries its own retort in an age which understands a little better just how romantic all the talk of the finality and precision of science was. The truth is that there is no substitute for Utopia and no substitute for hope, and that the moment men give up the right to invent, however extravagantly, their own future and submit themselves, as the communists and the capitalists tell them they must, to inevitable economic law, the life goes out of them. The democratic ideal is despised by the

Marxians as a foolish and improbable aspiration too lofty for the actual facts of life, but the actual facts of the Marxian substitute have failed to catch the imaginations of any but the most cruelly oppressed and injured men.

Let no man miss the point of Mr. Roosevelt's hold upon the minds of the citizens of this republic. Men's minds are fired by Mr. Roosevelt because they are sick to nausea of the rich bankers and their economists upon the one side and the wise revolutionaries and their economists upon the other, repeating over and over that the world is ruled by incontrovertible economic laws which it is not only blasphemy but idiocy to oppose, and which lead inevitably to certain fixed and inescapable conclusions. It is not the first time the world has been told it existed in a closed system of which the rules were comprehensible only to the doctors. And from the human point of view it is almost irrelevant whether or not Mr. Roosevelt's particular attempt to break out of the cage is successful. What is important is the attempt — and the reaction to that attempt on the part of the people of this nation. It is only to the free, inventive gestures of the human soul that men wholly and believingly respond. They will, in a crisis, rise against arrogance. They may, for a time, fight from hatred. But only to hope will they give themselves entirely. And only writers writing out of hope can lead them to anything more permanent than the barricades.

April, 1934.

OF THE LIBRARIAN'S PROFESSION

NOTHING is more difficult for the beginning librarian than to discover in what profession he is engaged. Certain professions define themselves. Others are defined by those who practice them. The librarian's profession is of neither nature. A librarian is so called not for what he does, as the farmer who farms or the lawyer who laws, but from the place in which he does it. And the definitions of the librarians, though they are eloquent in describing the librarian's perfections, are reticent in saying what the librarian's perfections are for.

Hugo Blotius, the sixteenth-century librarian of the Hofbibliothek in Vienna, defined his profession by saying that a librarian should be learned in languages, diligent and quiet — adding, by way of reminder to his master, the Emperor, that 'if not of noble blood he should be given a title to enhance the dignity of his office.' Cotton des Houssayes told the general assembly of the Sorbonne in 1780 that when he reflected 'on the qualifications that should be united in your librarian' they presented themselves to his mind in so great a number, and in such character of perfection, that he distrusted his ability not only to enumerate but even to trace a true picture of them.

Pressing himself to the point, however, the learned orator (who spoke, it should be noted, in the Latin tongue) supplied the following description of the office: 'Your librarian should be, above all, a learned and profound theologian; but to this qualification, which I shall call fundamental, should be united vast literary acquisitions, an exact and precise knowledge of all the arts and sciences, great facility of expression, and lastly, that exquisite politeness which conciliates the affection of his visitors while his merit secures their esteem.'

One gathers that M. des Houssayes thought well of the librarian's office, but beyond that, and a certain conviction of personal inadequacy, one is little wiser than before. To be at once a profound and learned theologian, the possessor of vast literary acquisitions, the exact and precise master of all the arts and all the sciences, a facile writer and a charming gentleman possessed of that exquisite politeness which wins heads as well as hearts, is to be an unusual and admirable human being — but even to be all these things at once is scarcely a profession.

And yet it is largely in the vein of the orator of the Sorbonne and the librarian of the Hofbibliothek that the profession of the librarian is presented. Modern librarians — perhaps because they do not speak in Latin — have never been as eloquent as Cotton des Houssayes, but even modern librarians write as though the profession of the librarian had been defined when the scholarly attainments and linguistic achievements of the, perhaps, ideal librarian have been described.

The consequence is that the beginning librarian is thrown upon his own resources, upon the dictionary, and upon the familiar sentences of the great founder of the Bodleian Library at Oxford. From Sir Thomas Bodley, besides learning that a librarian should not be 'encumbered with marriage nor with a benefice of cure' and that he should be 'a personable scholler and qualified, if it may be, with a gentlemanlike speeche and carriage . . . able to interteine commers in aswel of other nations as our owne, with meete discourses for the place,' the apprentice librarian will learn that a librarian is a keeper of a library. From the dictionary he will learn that a library is 'a large collection of books, public or private.' And by his own resources he will attempt to deduce what the keeper of a large collection of books, public or private, may, in actionable and intelligible language, be. Keeper, but how a keeper? Of books — but what, then, in this context is a book?

It is not an altogether simple question, and for this reason. There are two meanings of the word 'book,' and two relations, therefore, between a book and the man entrusted with its keeping. There is one meaning which signifies a physical object made of certain physical materials in a physical shape. There is another meaning which signifies an intellectual object made of all materials or of no materials and standing in as many shapes as there are forms and balances and structures in men's minds. The two meanings overlap and are confused. Readers associate the intellectual book with the physical book, thinking of Plato's vision of the world in terms of dark green linen and a gilded name. Collectors associate the physical book with the intellectual book, imagining that because they possess a rare edition of a poet's work they somehow have possessed the poem. But the two meanings are nevertheless distinct. The physical book is never more than an ingenious and often beautiful cipher by which the intellectual book is communicated from one

27

mind to another, and the intellectual book is always a structure in the imagination which may hang for a time above a folio page in ten-point type with a half-calf binding only to be found thereafter on a different page above a different type and even in another language.

When it is said, therefore, that a librarian is a keeper of books, it must be determined first of which of these two books he is the keeper. Is he, for one example, the keeper of the small, clothbound object of 110 pages of text and 6 of front matter manufactured by Macmillan & Co., Ltd., in London in 1928 and called *The Tower*, by W. B. Yeats? Or is he the keeper of that very different object created in many men's minds before, and now in yours, by this — these words, these symbols, images, perceptions —

> That is no country for old men. The young
> In one another's arms, birds in the trees,
> — Those dying generations — at their song,
> The salmon falls, the mackerel-crowded seas,
> Fish, flesh or fowl, commend all summer long
> Whatever is begotten born and dies.
> Caught in that sensuous music all neglect
> Monuments of unaging intellect.

It makes a difference whether the book is the cloth and paper or the intellectual image. If it is the physical book of which a librarian is keeper, then the character of his profession is obvious enough. He is a custodian as all keepers of physical objects are custodians, and his obligations are a custodian's obligations. He is a sort of check boy in the parcel room of culture. His duty is to receive the priceless packages confided to him by the past and to redeliver them to the future against the proper stub. To perform that obligation he must be reliable, orderly, industrious, and clever. He must devise infallible and complicated ticket systems to find the parcels on the shelves. He must read the notations of origin and ownership in a dozen tongues. He must guard the wrappers from the risks of time and theft and matches and men's thumbs. He must be courteous and patient with the claimants. And for the rest he has no duty but to wait. If no one comes, if no one questions, he can wait.

But if it is not the physical book but the intellectual book of which the librarian is keeper, then his profession is a profession of a very different kind. It is not the profession of the custodian, for the intellectual book is not a ticketed parcel which can be preserved by keeping it from mice and mildew on a shelf. The intellectual book is an imagined object in the mind which can be preserved only by preserving the mind's perception of its presence. Neither is the librarian's profession the profession of the check boy who receives and guards and redelivers — receives from the past, guards against the present, and redelivers to the future — for the intellectual book is not a deposit of the past which the future has a right to call and claim. The intellectual book is a construction of the spirit, and the constructions of the spirit exist in one time only — in that continuing and endless present which is now. If it is the intellectual book rather than the physical book of which the librarian is keeper, then the profession of the librarian is not and cannot be the neutral, passive, negative profession of the guardian and fiduciary, but must become instead the affirmative and advocating profession of the attorney for a cause. For the intellectual book is the word. And the keepers of the word, whether they so choose or not, must be its partisans and advocates. The word was never yet protected by keeping it in storage in a warehouse: the preservation of the word is now, as it has always been, a cause — perhaps the greatest — not, I think, the least in danger in this time.

It makes a difference, therefore — a very considerable difference in the understanding of the librarian's profession — which of these two meanings of the book is taken. Both are held. The librarian who asserts that the sole and single strength of his profession in a distracted world is its disinterested objectivity, meaning its negative and custodial detachment from the dangers which beset the Word, thinks of the book necessarily as a physical object on his shelves for which, in its intellectual aspects, he accepts no share of risk or credit. The library trustee or the moralizing editor who demands of librarians that they stick to the job of pasting on the labels and handing out the loans accepts, but with less honesty, the same assumption — less honesty because he speaks, not from love of the librarian's profession, but from hatred of the Word, and fear of its persuasions.

Those who love the power of the Word and who defend it take the opposite position. Shortly after William Dugard was released, through the efforts of John Milton, from Newgate prison, he published two letters by John Dury, deputy keeper in 1649 of the King's medals and library, which put the case with eagerness and passion: 'For if librairie-keepers did understand themselves in the nature of their work, and would make themselves, as they ought to bee, useful in their places in a publick waie; they ought to become agents for the advancement of universal learning. . . . The end of that imploiment, in my conception, is to keep the publick stock of learning, which is in books and mss., to increas it, and to propose it to others in the waie which may bee most useful unto all. His work then is to bee a factor and trader for helps to learning, and

30

a treasurer to keep them, and a dispenser to applie them to use or to see them well used, or at least not abused.'

As between these two conceptions of the profession, a man can choose only for himself and not for those who practice the profession with him. But there are, notwithstanding, certain considerations which even a novice among librarians may propose. The chief of these considerations is the nature of the times in which men live. In a different time from ours — such a time as men a generation ago considered natural and normal — it made relatively little difference whether a librarian behaved himself as a custodian of volumes or as a 'factor and trader for helps to learning, and a treasurer to keep them, and a dispenser to apply them to use.' A generation ago the word, the life of the mind, the monuments of unaging intellect, were not under attack. It was agreed by all civilized nations, by all governments in power, that the cultural tradition was a common treasure, that truth was an end to be sought equally by all men, and that the greatest glory and final justification of human life was the creativeness of the human spirit. In such a world the librarian who considered himself a custodian, who devoted himself to the perfection of his catalogue and the preservation of his bindings, and who waited for the calls of those who had business with his collections, was not only prudent but entirely wise. There was no need for him to advocate the cause of learning or to assert the supreme importance of the contents of his library, for no one doubted the one or challenged the other. The librarian who presented himself in the years before the Great War as a champion of culture would have received the ironic welcome he deserved. What was required of him then — and what he practiced — was discretion, dignity, and a judicial calm.

31

But the world in which we live is not that world. The world in which we live is a world that world would have believed impossible. In the world in which we live it is no longer agreed by all governments and citizens that truth is the final measure of men's acts and that the lie is shameful. There are governments abroad, and there are citizens here to whom respect for truth is naïve — governments and individuals who, when it is proved they lie, have not been shamed 'either in their own or in their neighbors' eyes.' In the world in which we live it is no longer agreed that the common culture is a common treasure. There are governments abroad, and there are citizens here to whom the common culture which draws the peoples of the West together is a common evil for which each nation must now substitute a private culture, a parochial art, a local poetry, and a tribal worship. In the world in which we live it is no longer agreed that the greatest glory and final justification of human history is the life of the human mind. To many men and many governments the life of the human mind is a danger to be feared more than any other danger, and the word which cannot be purchased, cannot be falsified, and cannot be killed is the enemy most hunted for and hated. It is not necessary to name names. It is not necessary to speak of the burning of the books in Germany, or of the victorious lie in Spain, or of the terror of the creative spirit in Russia, or of the hunting and hounding of those in this country who insist that certain truths be told and who will not be silent. These things are commonplaces. They are commonplaces to such a point that they no longer shock us into anger. Indeed it is the essential character of our time that the triumph of the lie, the mutilation of culture, and the persecution of the word no longer shock us into anger.

What those who undertake to keep the libraries must consider — or so it seems to me — is whether this profound and troubling alteration of the times alters also their profession. Granted that it was not only possible but desirable for the librarian to think of his profession in negative and custodial terms in the quiet generations when the burning of books was a medieval memory, is it still possible for librarians to think of their profession in these passive terms in a time in which the burning of the books is a present fact abroad and a present possibility at home?

Granted that it was not only prudent but wise as well for the librarian to admit no positive, affirmative duty to the cause of learning in a time when learning was universally honored and the works of great art and great scholarship were admired monuments, is it still wise for librarians to admit no positive duty to learning in a time when governments abroad teach ignorance instead of knowledge to their people, and fanatical and frightened citizens at home would, if they could, obliterate all art and learning but the art and learning they consider safe?

In a division which divides all men, because it is a division drawn through everything that men believe, can those who keep the libraries — those who keep the records of belief — avoid division? In a struggle which is truly fought, whatever the economic interpreters and the dialectical materialists may say to the contrary, across the countries of the spirit, can those who hold those countries remain neutral? In an attack which is directed, as no attack in history ever was directed, against the intellectual structures of the books, can those who keep the books contend their books are only objects made of print and paper?

I can answer only for myself. To me the answer is not doubtful. To me the changes of the time change everything. The obligations of the keepers of the books in such a time as ours are positive obligations because they have no choice but to be positive. Whatever the duty of the librarian may have been in a different world and a more peaceful generation, his duty now is to defend — to say, to fight, and to defend. No one else — neither those who make the books nor those who undertake to teach them — is bound as he is bound to fight in their behalf, for no one else is charged as he is charged with their protection. No one as much as he must say, and say again, and still insist that the tradition of the written word is whole and single and entire and cannot be dismembered. No one is under obligation as he is under obligation to meet the mutilators of the word, the preachers of obscurantism, the suppressors — those who would cut off here and ink out there the texts their prejudices or their parties or their churches or their fears find hateful. And these obligations are not obligations which are satisfied by negatives. The books can be protected from the preaching demagogues and the official liars and the terrorizing mob not by waiting for attack but by forestalling it. If the cultural tradition, the ancient and ever-present structure of the mind, can still be saved, it can be saved by reconstructing its authority. And the authority of art and learning rests on knowledge of the arts and learnings. Only by affirmation, only by exhibiting to the people the nobility and beauty of their intellectual inheritance, can that inheritance be made secure.

Some years before his elevation to the bench Mr. Justice Brandeis referred to himself as 'counsel for the situation.' The librarian in our time, or so it seems to me, becomes the counsel for the situation. His client is the inherited culture entrusted to his care. He — he more than any other man — must represent this client as its advocate. Against those who would destroy the tradition he must bring the force of the tradition. Against those who would mutilate the monuments he must bring the beauty of the monuments. Against those who would limit the freedom of the inquiring mind he must bring the marvels of the mind's discoveries.

Keepers of books, keepers of print and paper on the shelves, librarians are keepers also of the records of the human spirit — the records of men's watch upon the world and on themselves. In such a time as ours, when wars are made against the spirit and its works, the keeping of these records is itself a kind of warfare. The keepers, whether they so wish or not, cannot be neutral.

June, 1940.

MR. SANDBURG AND THE
DOCTRINAIRES

EVEN a non-book-reviewer may take advantage
of the book-reviewer's figure of speech with Carl
Sandburg's *The People, Yes*. *The People, Yes*
ought to be required reading for every man in
every American metropolis who calls himself a revolutionary. It will teach him something. It will teach him that
the tradition of the people and the land is not dead in this
republic. It will teach him, further, that that tradition is
the one tradition upon which he can build if he wishes to
build a social revolution which will succeed.

The revolutionary movement in America at the present
is in a very unenviable position. It has missed the lives
of the people. The reason is well known to everyone who
remembers the last fifteen years. Fifteen years ago American radicals believed Mencken when he wrote of the great
American boob. They did not perceive that Mencken,
in sneering at the boobocracy, was sneering also at the
people, nor that Mencken, in ridiculing the Owners, was
doing the Owners' work. All that is clear now. It is clear
now that the weakening of the American faith in American
democracy did not lead, as was foolishly hoped, to the
substitution of a different democracy, but to the threat of
democracy's opposite. Mencken is now highly visible in

his own colors. It is apparent that his actual effect was to poison the belief of the people in themselves and to forward the kind of cynical and violent suppression of the people which is now preparing.

But fifteen years ago it was not clear. Fifteen years ago the people were fools and the democratic tradition was dead and the only thing to be done was to introduce a new tradition of world revolution stated in hard-headed, realistic terms. The intelligent men, the leaders, realized that the democratic tradition must also be part of the tradition of any revolution to be made in America, but the run of American radicals in the twenties threw out the baby with the bath. American history was for the D.A.R. Their revolution would make its own history.

That kind of talk was harmless as long as the radical movement, coasting on the impulse of the war, retained the offensive: the others were nervous and diffident and there was nothing much to be feared but the Red-baiters. It ceased to be harmless when the others recovered their courage and took back the offensive in Italy and then in Germany and then elsewhere. When that happened, radical leaders in America began to take stock of the actual situation. What they discovered did not comfort them. The tough, realistic twig of world revolution which had been brought into America two or three generations before by courageous and hopeful men was still a twig kept alive in water. It had not been grafted to the tree. Until it was grafted to the tree it would put forth no leaves.

It was then that attempts began to be made to notch the twig into the American past. First chosen was the past of the American Revolution. The Washington Elm and the Charter Oak were to be claimed for the true democratic revolution which had collapsed when Hamilton seized power and which was now to be revived. It was a just and honorable attempt and it failed to succeed only because every American political candidate who ever shouted over a jug of water on a schoolhouse desk had made precisely the same claim for himself. American candidates and American parties have always been the true heirs of the founding fathers, and the radical movement, in making the same claim for itself, merely joined a long and none too honorable procession. It made no difference that the twig of revolution notched perfectly into the great American elm of 1776. The great American elm of 1776 had been hauled off by the Davey Tree Surgeons to the green lawn of the duPonts and the heavy branches had been trimmed down to shade a well-bred cocktail party of the Very Few.

We find ourselves still in that dilemma. We hold in our hands the growing thing, the true shelter for a great people and yet it will neither grow nor shelter until it is grafted to the green wood of the people's lives. It is to us, and at this time, that Sandburg speaks. What he says to those who have attempted to spell the name of their own cause out of the cracked letters of the Liberty Bell is this: Why turn back? Why say the people were right *then?* Why not say the people are right still?

'The people,' said a farmer's wife in a Minnesota country store where her husband was buying a new post-hole digger. 'The people,' she went on, 'will stick around a long time.'

What he says to those who talk and write in the cities is this: Why not know the people? There are many men in the great cities in America who do not know the people. There are also many men in the great cities who do not understand that it is necessary, in order to know the people,

38

to know their country. The people in America as in any other country are bred as well of the land as of their fathers and mothers. Because the Nazis have made much of this relation it does not follow that it is not a relation which exists. If every human emotion to which Hitler has laid particular claim is to be surrendered to him, the revolution will have to express itself in the abstract symbols of pure mathematics. I remember being told recently by a group of young men at City College that love of the land was a childish emotion to be put aside with childhood. Intellectualism and faint-heartedness could scarcely go farther. People belong to their countrysides. There is a story told of two New York photographers of great skill who went out into the Plains to make a moving picture of the life of the farmers and who expected to find there the peasants of whom they had read in books on Russia and who were disillusioned and angry to find that the farmers of the Plains were not peasants at all, but something very different for which they could discover no word in their books.

What Sandburg does first of all for these men in the great cities is to show them the people against the land.

> and in the shivering cold they say
>   'Between Amarilla and the North Pole
>   is only a barbwire fence,'

And again:

> The people know what the land knows
> the numbers odd and even of the land
> the slow hot wind of summer and its withering
> or again the crimp of the driving white blizzard
> and neither of them to be stopped
> neither saying anything else than:
>   'I'm not arguing. I'm telling you.'

What he does next is to show them the people themselves. He does not pretend to superior knowledge.

> Who shall speak for the people?
> Who knows the works from A to Z so he can say,
>   'I know what the people want'?   Who is this phenom?
>   where did he come from?

He shows the people in their language, in their proverbs, in the hang of their talk, in the twists of thinking which are peculiarly theirs. Out of the book comes the true smell and sound of humanity, the warm, endless, unending movement of men. It is the smell and the sound and the movement of all men everywhere. But it is also the smell and the sound and the movement of men on this continent. Out of the book comes for the first time in our literature the people of America. Whitman's men were Man. Sandburg's are men of this earth. It has taken our generation a long time to admit that we were not only a nation but a *people*. Now we are. The People. Yes.

But what Sandburg does for us particularly is more even than that. He points out the living tree to which the branch may be grafted. He points out the one great tradition in American life strong enough and live enough to carry the revolution of the oppressed. That tradition is the belief *in* the people. That is the tree against which the cat-calling satirists of the twenties broke their claws.

America has always been dedicated in words to the belief in the people. The revolution against England was made by men who believed in the people — who were the people. But that dedication in words has always been betrayed in fact. The men who wrote the Constitution did not believe in the people and only the power of Jefferson and his friends prevented them from rooting out of their document every generous and democratic word.

Into the Constitution of the United States they wrote a fear
In the form of 'checks and balances,' 'proper restraints'
On the people so whimsical and changeable,
So variable in mood and weather....

Men of 'solid substance' wore velvet knickerbockers
And shared snuff with each other in greetings.
One of these made a name for himself with saying
You could never tell next what was coming from the people:
'Your people, sir, your people is a great beast,'
Speaking for those afraid of the people....

For better than a century, in the Supreme Court and
in the Congress the country has been ruled by those who
did not believe in the people. Men like Lincoln who did
believe were used by those who came after them, as Lincoln
has been used by the owners of the Republican Party, to
polish up the Big Words for the further deceit of the citizens. For a hundred years and more the country has been
ruled by those who used the language of belief in the people
to exploit the people. And yet through all that time, says
Sandburg, the belief of the people in themselves has en-
dured. It is alive. It is strong. It needs only the new
branch to leaf out and be green.

The revolutionary party which can support that belief
and give it new form, the revolutionary party which can
offer to restore the government to the people and which
can convince the people of its sincerity in so offering, the
revolutionary party which can bring to pass the great
American dream of the commonwealth, the people's state
— that revolutionary party will inherit the history of this
country and change it into truth.

September 1, 1936.

THE POETRY OF KARL MARX

WHEN the parties to a controversy begin to discuss each other it is usually safe to assume that the controversy is dead. The red herring is a bird of ambiguous lineage which has been known to put on various shapes. Not the least common of which is personal affront.

It is permissible to hope, however, that the recent discussion of the rôle of the poet in our time may not be as defunct as the barrage of epithets would lead one to suppose. It has been a useful discussion. It has revived — and for this the dialecticians deserve the praise — a journalistic interest in poetry which the prosperous twenties had done their best to kill. And it has produced, also, among the Marxians, a certain amount of skillful invective which even its victims must admire. But the real issue, either because the controversialists would not see it or because they could not, remains untouched.

Serious discussion has been pretty much confined to two heads of argument: the contention that propaganda is, or is not, art, and the contention that only the poet who 'soaks himself in the historic necessities of his epoch' can write good poetry. Of these the first is irrelevant to the actual issue and the second is only superficially pertinent.

The argument which opposes art to propaganda is merely no argument. There are no *a priori* rules about

subject matter in verse and the man who contends that
there are is either an academician or that equally unimportant American phenomenon, the revolutionary pedant.
Anything which will make a work of art will make a work
of art. It is just as silly to say that a poem can't be a poem
if its subject is The Young Communists as it is to say
that a poem can't be a poem *unless* its subject is The
Young Communists. It is just as ridiculous to assert that
the time and place of a poem must be here and now as
it is to assert that the only proper subject for an epic is
the rape of Troy. The fact is, as a glance at the (politi-
cally) left-wing magazines will immediately show, that
revolutionary content has precisely nothing to do with
poetry one way or the other. Where the writer is an
honest workman and where he is deeply moved in his own
person, his revolutionary verses may be poems. Where
the writer is a dishonest workman or where he is substi-
tuting for his own emotion the emotion of a Movement,
his revolutionary verses are never poems. But the same
thing is true of a lady sonneteer writing about her Lost
Loves. All that can intelligently be said of either is that
there is no substitute for art — not even fervor. To criticize a writer because he does, or does not, write of the
political issues of his day is to risk playing a ridiculous
rôle before a posterity which may value the writing long
after the issues have, for generations, been forgotten. A
poem called *To Daffodils* and a book entitled *Leviathan*
are cases decidedly in point.

The second contention on the other hand — the contention that only the poet who soaks himself in the historic
necessities of his epoch can write good poetry on any
subject — is a proper matter of debate but one which
proves ultimately to lead into a *cul-de-sac*. Even if the

truth of the proposition is admitted over the protests of
the students of English verse, it still remains to inquire:
What historic necessities and by whom determined? I, for
one, am strongly inclined to believe that the contention
may be truer of our time than it was of the time of Robert
Herrick or William Blake or Shakespeare himself. But I
am not willing to agree that the bath in which the contemporary poet is to soak is the bath in which I see certain
of the proponents of this view actually soaking. To soak
oneself in books, to soak oneself in dialectic, to soak oneself
in theory, is still to soak oneself in books and dialectic and
theory whether the books and the theories are those of a
graduate school of English or those of a school of political
revolution. And the results will be the same — pedantry,
academicism, intellectualism, and very bad poetry: the
kind of poetry precisely which the intellectuals, both col-
legiate and revolutionary, do now so frequently produce.

What the poet must soak himself in, if he is to take to
soaking, is his own time and not theories about his time,
and particularly not theories about his time developed
almost a hundred years before and in another country.
Now, the outstanding characteristic of our time is industrialism. Whether modern society is run from Wall
Street or the Kremlin, it is still first and foremost an industrial society — indeed its industrialism is if anything
more emphatic in Russia than in the United States. But
industrialism is not a theory. It is a condition. It is a fact.
It is a highly technical mechanism of complicated and
difficult controls which exists only in its operation, only
as a thing in action. It is so far fundamental that if it
should collapse all issues of capitalism and socialism and
proletarianism would be swept away together in a common
disaster which would reduce the question of the control

of the instruments of production to the inanity of the
Nestorian heresy. Only those, therefore, who understand
industrialism as an existing, working physical mechanism
can lay any claim whatever to an understanding of our
time. The rest, those who assume industrialism and debate
the question merely of its control, are as infantile as
children who assume that dinners appear upon tables as
a matter of natural right and that the only question is
who shall get the largest helping. And those whose sole
knowledge of the contemporary world is a knowledge of
its social injustice belong, for all the generosity of their
indignation, to the same category. For it is not social injustice which is the peculiar characteristic of our time.
It is social injustice bred by industrialism.

It follows that the man who really proposes to soak himself in his time will soak himself not in books but in industrialism as a reality, as a physical, existing fact. And
yet I know of no poetic champions of the historic necessity
doctrine who have made the slightest attempt to do so.
They have read Marx. They have soaked themselves in
the rancid odor of capitalistic stupidity and greed. They
have looked at, and romantically admired, and even romantically written about, a few esthetic-looking machines
and tools. But they have no faintest idea how three hundred odd millions of pairs of shoes are actually made under
any social system or how the food of a nation is actually
distributed — actually: the visible, tangible, physical act
— or by what organization of men and railroads and trucks
and belts and book-entries the materials of a single automobile are assembled. And yet all these matters are of
the very life of our time. They are the facts upon which
theories must rest. And for the poet, who must always
attack his world factually and physically, not abstractly,

45

not in intellectual concepts, they are the one possible road to an understanding of the contemporary age. Those who refuse that road, who do not so much soak themselves in the actual liquor of their time as vaporize in its theories, must face the suspicion that their loyalties are less to the historic necessities of their generation than to the dogmas of their church.

It will be replied, of course, that this is not at all what the words 'historic necessity' connote: that the words 'historic necessity' refer to the natural laws of social evolution discovered by Karl Marx — the social trend, the direction of the time. But the only kind of contemporary history in which the poet, the artist, the essentially practical man who makes books and paintings and music, can possibly immerse himself to the advantage of himself or his art is the present history of the existing world. All the rest is *Zeit-Geist*, Spirit of the Age — and as Teutonic and romantic as *The Sorrows of Werther*.

The fundamental point to be made, however, is that the theory of the historic necessity leaves the real question of the rôle of the poet in our epoch quite untouched. The real question is not whether the poet should know and draw upon the existing world of his time, but whether he should know and draw upon that world as an artist with an artist's single and arrogant demand of artistic significance or as a partisan with the ulterior and calculated interest of the champion of a cause. Briefly the real question is whether the poet should serve a cause or serve an art. It is a question which every man attempting to practice the art of poetry in this time must answer. And which he must answer with the certainty that he will choose one alternative or the other and cannot possibly choose both. There may be cakes in the political world which can be both kept and eaten. There are none in the world of art.

It cannot be too often repeated that this issue and the issue of propaganda with which the Marxians attempt, for some reason, to confuse it are not at all the same. Propaganda is a question of the subject matter of particular poems. The question here at issue concerns the art itself, the lens through which the light should come. Ultimately and inescapably it is a question of the relative importance of the art of poetry upon the one hand and on the other the cause to which that art would be deferred.

There are those who believe that the importance of the art of poetry, even from the social point of view which is now so generally imposed, is very great. The modern world, obviously, does not share that opinion. The modern world conceives of itself as depending upon its scientists for a knowledge of the external universe and upon its psychologists for a knowledge of the internal mind and upon itself for everything else of which it has need. But the modern world is deceived. Neither in our day nor at any earlier time has the world been able to depend upon itself for its essential understanding. A great part of our racial knowledge of our lives and our earth and our destiny upon that earth has come in all ages from the intuitive and emotional perceptions of great poets.

The poet works with those dimensions of invisibility which exist at the opposite extreme from the microscopic dimensions which concern the scientist. He works with the over-obvious, the too-apparent, the phenomena which men cannot see because they are so close that vision blurs, the phenomena which approach the seeing eye so near that they become sometimes the seeing eye itself. It is for this reason that the true perceptions of the poet have such an overwhelming and instantaneous feel of truth. They require no demonstration because they were always true. They were merely never 'seen' before. The poet, with the adjustment of a phrase, with the contrast of an image, with the rhythm of a line, has fixed a focus which all the talk and all the staring of the world had been unable to fix before him. His is a labor which is at all times necessary, for without it that sense of human reality which is the poet's greatest accomplishment is lost. But it is a labor which is particularly necessary in times of uncertainty and doubt and intellectual confusion. No man who lived through the publication of *The Waste Land* will forget the crystallizing effect of that poem, the way in which it precipitated the cloudy confusion of an age, and made human and tragic what had before been impersonal and intellectual and for the most part unseen.

The importance, even the social importance, of the art of poetry will therefore hardly be challenged by any save the ignorant. But the truth to be driven home is not that the poet is important. The truth to be driven home is that the poet is important only so long as he acts as poet. The reason is the same as the reason which explains a similar limitation upon the importance of the scientist. The reports of the scientist upon the nature of the physical world are accepted as the bases for conclusions and the grounds for action for one reason only — because the scientist is disinterested. And the scientist is disinterested because his loyalty is to his science. He has no ulterior motive. He has not committed himself to certain extra-scientific views which condition all his findings. He has no preconceptions as to what he would like to find to be true. In the same way the intuitions of the poet are valid and may be accepted only because his loyalty is to his art, because his sole test of the acceptability of a word or a phrase or a poem is the test of his art and not the test of his politics or his social indignation. This is not to say that the true poet is without prejudice. He has of course the prejudices of his blood, his countryside, his education, if you will his 'class.' But the only demand to which he listens in the making of a poem, the only demand which, satisfied, will satisfy him that the poem is complete, is the demand which his art makes upon him. Where he fails in that, as all poets have frequently failed, he fails of poetry.

Those immature minds which dismiss all difficult facts with epithets will find in this truth nothing but the old, stale doctrine of Art-for-Art's sake. And the use of the phrase will somehow comfort them. The rest, however, will remark that the difference between a man who serves an art and the man who serves a cause is an actual difference. The servant of a cause accepts of necessity certain preconceptions as to the nature and meaning of life and the quality of the world. He desires his experience to prove to him that his cause is just and will be successful. He rejects anything in his experience which suggests to him that his cause is unjust and will fail. He is a special pleader. And as such his work loses poetic authority because the guarantee of its validity is lost in the loss of the guarantee of his artistic disinterestedness. In the paintings of Cézanne every sensitive man recognizes the profound authority of the artist by whom the world is truthfully presented because the world, to him, is merely material for his art. In the work of George Grosz the observer feels the partisan and interested presentation of a skilled and passionate pleader.

These are the two alternatives of our time. All writers

who hate the stupidity and insolence and inhumanity of the existing order must choose between them. But they must choose with the full and certain knowledge that the alternatives are actually alternatives: that it is impossible to be both Cézanne and Grosz. A few honest men have made the choice of partisanship with their eyes open and in full recognition of the meaning of their act. Unable themselves to live as poets in a house in which the drains were clogged, they have generously elected to clear the drains for the next tenant. Their decision must be respected and admired. But they are few. Beside them are the scores of frightened and bewildered writers who, unaware of the meaning of their choice, aware only that the practice of an art is today lonely and difficult, have escaped into the security of a Movement and the support of an organized claque. And beyond are the crowds of intellectualists and critics who, having no artistic obligations and hence no choice to make, shout for blood at the ringside like fat Long Island brokers at a ten-round bout.

There remain certain individuals who believe that the first and inescapable obligation of the poet is his obligation to his art; who believe that the fact that the practice of his art is difficult in no way releases him from that obligation; who believe that the desertion of his art for any reason, even the noblest, even the most humane, is nevertheless desertion. Neither they nor any other honest writers will ignore the issues of their time. On the contrary they will know their time as well as it is possible for them to know it. They will write of their time either explicitly or by indirection as all serious men always write of their time whatever the scene or subject of their work. They will, when they so incline, write propaganda if their propaganda satisfies the necessities under which, as poets, they must work. But they will admit no loyalty before the single loyalty they owe their art.

Time which survives the generations and the causes, time in which alone the work of art exists, will damn them or commend them at its leisure.

February, 1934.

NEVERTHELESS ONE DEBT

A GREAT change in the world is to the poet a very great danger. It is not necessarily a danger to the rest of us. The great majority of people can go on living in a world which has ceased to exist with no inconvenience whatever. Lawyers and politicians are adepts at the practice. They can go in and out of doors that have been down for generations. And even the hardest-headed industrialists will go on vaulting at an imaginary hurdle like a file of sheep — until one of them accidentally walks through and the rest of them take the short cut after him. But the poet lives in a very curious relation to the world. He is condemned to prefer the imitation of life to life itself. He can satisfy the needs of his nature only by laboring to fix in some artificial substance of sounds and signs a moment, an aspect, of the flowing away of the world.

Like the fabulous gorgons, he can seize only by turning to stone. Only in its images can he possess his life. If he attempts to take it at first hand, to live it himself, to go along with it, to lose himself in it, he is eaten with shame and remorse. His conscience wakes him. He feels that he and everything about him are crumbling and dissolving away to no purpose and with no end. His whole life is like those moments we all endure in the spring and the fall of the year when the change of the earth is so apparent to us and so poignant that we cannot watch it — that we try to arrest it for ourselves by calling others to see it, to stand looking at it, to be still beside us seeing it.

All the poet's art is the product of that relation of a man to a world — good as that relation is close and is actual, bad as that relation is loose and false. Consequently the poet who goes on living in a world which has stopped is merely and precisely a fool. He is arresting with a great flourish of eloquence the fleeting gesture of an iron deer. He is throwing open the windows of the soul upon a stage drop. He is imitating the imitation of an imitation. He is doing the one thing that it is not lawful for him to do.

I do not, of course, mean to suggest that the poet who places the action of his poetry in a time prior to his own, or in another country, is a fool. The poet who seems to me to write most profoundly of the world in which we now so blindly find ourselves (more profoundly by many fathoms than the gentlemen whose poems dress themselves in the properties of the contemporary age) is a Frenchman born in Martinique who uses the scenes and times of pastoral Asia. And most of the great poets of the English tradition have written the experiences of their lives into other times, and into countries equally remote — Italian cities, Danish castles, Egypt, and the plains of heaven itself. The *mis-en-scène* is not important. It is merely one of the elements which act to disengage the poem. What is important is that the poem should respond to a living world. It is a mystery if you will. There is no plain reason why a twentieth-century poem responding to the world of Marie de France should not be a good poem, as good as any of her own *lais*. But it is perfectly certain that it will not be.

In most generations, in the generations in which poetry thrives but not always in the generations in which it is most interesting, there is no difficulty about identifying the living world. It has been defined by others before, it has been explored, it is well known, it is taken for granted. But in an age of revolution and change the difficulty is profound. And it is increased by the fact that the great majority refuse to see for themselves that anything whatever is different, and resent irritably being told. Our own is, of course, such an age. The names of the change are legion: what they intend is the fact that the society of the western world has become, after a century in process, an industrialized society. Industrialization means a great many things, but chiefly it means an alteration in the status of the individual. The individual is no longer the unit, the sacred integer, the solemn end. He is a fraction. He is an agent.

Society, which was organized for his happiness and his protection in accordance with the philosophical views of the eighteenth century, has been reorganized for his employment as an industrial factor in accordance with the necessities of the industrial state. The forms of the French Revolution still remain. We talk about our rights and our freedom as though we still had them, and we maintain republican and democratic governments as though they existed still. But we are actually the least independent of creatures. We can do nothing by ourselves. If society should leave us alone, we would starve. We can eat and sleep and wear clothes only if we eat and sleep and wear clothes all together. Laws which were made, and which still pretend, to prevent us from interfering with each other in the free exercise of our individual right to do as we please, are now enforced to bring us as closely together into a common and efficient activity as possible.

Even those who do no work are fitted into the gears. There were formerly on this earth producers, middle-men, and consumers. There is now a closed circle with money flowing around it in one direction and goods flowing around it in the other, like the Panders and the Seducers in the Eighth Circle of Dante's Hell. If the manufacturer does not pump wages out on the one side, he will not be able to pump radios out on the other. And the obvious and soul-satisfying rôle of the good citizen is to buy in order that he may earn in order that he may buy. In other words, society has actually and not as a Christian figure of speech, and not at all in a manner agreeable to the Christians, become more important than the individual. The individual can only realize himself in his social rôle. And the few exceptions which wealth still permits in this country are artificial and unimportant. The United States may be as different from Soviet Russia in this regard as the politicians seem to think. But from the point of view of such an individualist as, say, Rabelais they would look astonishingly alike.

The obsequies of individualism bring to an end one of the great periods of human history — the period which had its beginning with the Renaissance. And they also bring to an end a literary tradition which has produced a considerable body of literature of the first order. Poetry, however, which in these matters is more sensitive than prose, and very much more sensitive than the professional observers of human progress, has been aware of the impending event for more than a hundred years. The individualistic self-consciousness of the Romantic Movement with

55

its Geniuses and its Heroes was a sign. So, too, but in a different way, was the nineteenth century of Baudelaire. Baudelaire was a poet turned inward upon the nerves and the emotions, and the poets who followed him were equally poets turned inward and away from the changing world. If they imitated the external, it was the Singular and the Strange they imitated. The spiritual microcosm of Rimbaud, the intellectual mirrors of Mallarmé, the gazing crystal of Parnasse, the religious doubts and classical escapes of Arnold and the English, are all aspects of the same thing. Poetry was aware of the impending event and refused it.

It could not, however, refuse forever to *see* what it so well divined. The change came with the present century. It took the form of a direct and excited recognition of the surfaces of the contemporary world, and, with Appollinaire and Cendars in France and Pound in England, a sort of willful and perverse assent to it. People talked about belonging to their own time and revolting against the old time. They made a great many experiments in form. They introduced words taken from the new vocabulary of the machine. They formed schools and founded magazines. It was a time of great artistic excitement in which a great many wise things and a great many foolish things were said. But it was a good time, and the people who made it were for the most part brave and honorable people. They bore the brunt of the turn of the century. They looked squarely at the world for the first time in a hundred years. They chose to be alive rather than to be dead. And any man now attempting to practice the art of poetry who forgets his obligation to them is ungrateful or ignorant. But though they looked at their own time, and though they wrote about it, their hearts were still in the other world. As the greatest of their poems proves. *The Waste Land* is a poem which sees the contemporary world as the wreckage and scattered ruin of many great and fallen cities, and Eliot's masterpiece, though its influence fell forward into the years which followed its publication, was actually a termination: a lament and a prayer. Nothing could follow it but darkness and silence. Or a new beginning.

It is that new beginning which constitutes the great poetic labor of our day — a labor which involves the acceptance of the change, not as the disastrous end of one mentality, but as the possible commencement of another. Unless poetry can not only perceive, but also *feel*, the race of men to be more important than any one man, we are merely fighting back against the water. And it is not an easy thing to feel. It involves the surrender of almost all our inherited and instinctive preferences. The Christian Church has taught us the phrases of altruism — they come so readily to our tongues that we think we consent to them. But the Christian Church also offered us the salvation of the self, whereas here no question either of altruism or of self is presented.

It is no longer A MAN against the stars. It is Mankind: that which has happened always to all men, not the particular incidents of particular lives. The common, simple, earth-riding ways of hands and feet and flesh against the enormous mysteries of sun and moon, of time, of disappearance-and-their-place-knowing-them-no-more. The salt-sweating, robust, passionate, and at the last death-devoured lives of all men always. Man in the invisible seas of time that drown him. Man in the sun, on the earth, under the branches — and, as he breathes, time sweeping him away. Not the 'great,' the 'leaders,' the brass-voices, but these men, these lives, and now death taking them. Not myself, my soul, my glycerine-dropping eyes, but these unknown and nameless men, anonymous under this sky, small in these valleys and far-off and forever there.

Poetry, which owes no man anything, owes nevertheless one debt — an image of mankind in which men can again believe. I do not know to whom this debt is owed or why.

July, 1931.

PUBLIC SPEECH AND PRIVATE
SPEECH IN POETRY

THE common significance of the poetry associated with the names of Yeats and Eliot and
Pound is a significance of language. Their work,
whether it was so intended or not, has had the
effect of regaining for poetry the public speech of which it
had been so long deprived. In effect if not in purpose it was
a revolt against the almost neurotic nineteenth-century
conception of poetry which had exiled poets from the actual world. It restored the conception of poetry in which a
poem, like a war or an edict, is an action on this earth.

There have been, of course, other and very different inter-
pretations of the significance of this poetry. Miss Lowell
and her friends, for example, understood that Ezra Pound
was attacking the rhetoric and the formalisms and the
'poetic language' of nineteenth-century British poetry.
They understood also that his hope was to compose a
poetry based upon the phrases of living speech, alive still
with the emphasis of breathing mouths. They failed,
however, to understand that it was insufficient merely to
release the good cloth of poetry from the silly starch of
nineteenth-century etiquette and convention and bad
taste. They did not understand that it was necessary also
to find for that released language a new form capable of
fixing and accentuating its living rhythms, and that Pound
had found that form. All forms in art are, from this point

of view at least, devices for catching the substance of experience in a timeless tension from which it cannot escape: within which it remains as though alive while yet incapable of death. Free Verse, because it could exert no pressure upon the rhythms it employed, because it had no means of increasing the tension of the line, was merely an abortive demonstration of the need for revolution. It was not the revolution itself.

The same thing is true of Eliot's theory of *The Tradition* and of his highly successful attempt to demonstrate the intellectual and moral relationship between the modern world and its past by building a modern poetry out of the distracted wreckage of poems long since made. The intellectual construction of *The Waste Land*, and the theories underlying that construction, have nothing to do with the significance of the poetry of *The Waste Land*, though they have a great deal to do with that very eminent modern poet Mr. T. S. Eliot. Indeed, they are in essence nothing but a kind of broken-hearted and ironic inversion of the almost universal practice of those earlier centuries in England and France when new poems (and a new age) were built quite candidly and believingly out of the broken stones of classical antiquity. The only functional difference between Eliot's classical allusions and Milton's is that Milton's stones were chosen to embellish the edifice he was building while Eliot's were chosen to betray the tragic shoddiness of his time. The great stones at Palmyra shoulder through the Arab huts with just such brutal and contemptuous despair.

The true significance of Eliot's poetry is not the characteristic architecture of his greatest poem. The true significance of Eliot's poetry is the lovely and living lucidity of the language Eliot has taken from the mouths of his contemporaries and fixed beyond the reach of time or anything in rhythms beautiful as they are difficult and difficult as they are sure.

The essential characteristic of the entire movement, properly so described, is this characteristic. It is poetry which has recovered the use of living tongues as Drayton had the use of living tongues when he wrote:

Since there's no help, come, let us kiss and part.

Or as the anonymous poet of the Western Wind had the use of living tongues when he said:

O western wind when wilt thou blow
That the small rain down can rain: —
Christ, that my love were in my arms
And I in my bed again.

But it would be a mistake, and a very serious mistake, to assume that this achievement is merely aesthetic — merely an achievement of vocabulary and rhythm, of ear and art. On the contrary, it is an achievement of much greater significance. For the recovery of the use of living tongues means that poetry can again reoccupy the living world from which it has been so long excluded. And the reoccupation of the living world by poetry means, with equal necessity, its reoccupation by poets. Which, in turn, means, or may mean, two things of some importance. It means an end to a conception of poetry which made that art a sort of costume ball for immature romantics: a place where no adult artist would be seen sober and alone. And it means the hope of a new and shaping influence in a world which needs, of all things, shape and meaning most.

Pound undoubtedly believed that the object of his hostility was the thing he said it was — a bourgeois conventionality of form in writing, a Philistine fear of actuality in experience: in brief, a rhetoric. Pound, it must be postulated, is one of those rarest and purest of poets whose approach to their art is that of the artist and of no one else. He is, moreover, a man to whom the problems of society present themselves schoolmaster-wise as problems of stupidity rather than poet-wise as problems of humanity. But it is, nevertheless, true, regardless of Pound's own description of the objective, that the source of poetic rhetoric is a rhetorical poet, that a rhetorical poet is the product of an age which expects poets to be rhetorical, and that the real conception to be destroyed was the nineteenth-century British conception of what a poet was.

Why precisely the nineteenth century painted for itself the extraordinary portrait of the poet with which we are all so unhappily familiar is a question for the historians of morbid psychology. Certainly the nineteenth-century poet, the private speaker, the whisperer to the heart, the unworldly romantic, the quaint Bohemian, the under-stander of women, the young man with the girl's eyes — certainly this poet was a ridiculous and pathetic figure to follow in the great line of Milton and Dante. From the beginning of literature the poets had been the proud free movers in the world: its lovers, its scholars, its observers. But this creature in the Italian cloak who stalked moodily through the minds of the British nineteenth century regarded The World with horror and disgust. From the beginning of literature the poets had attempted to understand at least as much of their time as their contemporaries for whom they described it. But this figure with the drooping thumbs was incapable, professionally incapable, of understanding what the most ignorant of stockbrokers was talking about. He would have considered himself no poet had he seen and understood the furnaces and the coalpits and the starving children of the Midlands, for his art permitted him to see only stars and maidens' breasts and pure-hearted kings and April flowers and pretty lakes and other countries under brighter suns. And yet his predecessors in Greece and Rome had written very little of flowers and moons and maidens. Instead they had written of governments and governors, of wars, of policies, of love (all forms of love), of gods (all varieties of gods), of death (many and different kinds of death). They had presented their time. They had asked and answered the most penetrating questions of their time. They had known more of their time — and not only of its spirit but of its economics and its politics — than those among whom they lived. They were capable of the world. They were able in the world. Their poetry was public speech. It reached conclusions.

And all this was true not only of those two civilizations of which we think when we think of such poetry — not only true of Greece and of Rome — but of Dante's Italy a thousand, two thousand years later, and of Chaucer's England and of Shakespeare's England and of Milton's and on down to Dryden's and even Pope's. The speech of all these poets was public speech. They knew — they would have been ashamed *not* to know — the meaning of their times better than the men who did not write could know them. They made no distinction between poetry and the world. Poetry was in the world, and the world was in poetry, and a man was better as a poet as he was more deeply and more understandingly and more naturally in the world. The notion that poetry was too fine for the world and that the world was too coarse for poetry was a notion which would have been as incomprehensible as it would have been shocking to the author of the *Areopagitica* and the author of *Richard II* and the author of *The Divine Comedy*.

And yet it existed in the British nineteenth century and

in our own. And why? Were the poets emasculated, as the Marxists would have us believe, by the desire, conscious or unconscious, of their masters, the new industrialists, to distract attention from the horrors of the textile mills: did they write about posies and the Church of England, and trips through the Hebrides and 'unhappy, far-off things' because the whole age was hypocritically committed to a policy of not understanding what was going on in the Midlands and in Egypt and in Africa and in India and in China? Were the poets driven out of the living world and forced to betray it by the piled-up pressures of Good Form and the Universities and the Best People? Or was it the poets themselves? Did the Industrial Revolution, by laying bare the baser economic nature of man, his greed, his dependence upon the hope of profit, his willingness to sweat his profit out of any living creature — did the Industrial Revolution so disgust the poets of the last century that they could not face the truth? Were they shocked and silenced by the discovery that the ritual and tradition and convention of the earlier world, which they had known and celebrated, covered such shallow graves? Or was it the rise of the novel? Did the greater muscularity and suppleness of prose move so easily in the world that the poets, in pique or in despair, were forced to leave it? Or was it perhaps some change in audience? Did the women's audience created by the Industrial Revolution among the women of the middle classes create in turn a poetry for women? Did the middle-class women, exiles themselves and often unwilling exiles from a world in which, a generation back, they had been workers, make companion exiles of the poets?

The speculations are infinite. All that is certain is the fact. Somehow and for some reason, the nineteenth century contrived for itself a portrait of the poet which was fit only for exhibition in a golden locket set about with once-blond hair. And somehow and for some reason, the nineteenth-century poet accepted the likeness. He was not taken seriously by the active men of his time, and he knew he was not taken seriously. That he suffered in consequence I think we must admit, for it has been possible in our own time to suffer from that same cause. The picture of the poet who was capable of writing Tennyson's *Ulysses* devoting his vigorous years to the tinting of the teacup china of *The Idylls of the King* is not a pleasant picture. Neither is it pleasant to think of later poets tied by the invisible wire of convention to a teacup art.

The poetry of Yeats and Eliot and Pound was, in a sense then, the breaking of the teacup. It was as insignificant an act as that. And yet the consequences have already been enormous and may be greater still. The consequences have been the return of poetry to the actual streets and doors and houses of our world and the return of the poet to a position of common responsibility among the men and women of his time. It would be self-deceiving to believe that the nineteenth-century picture of the poet has been erased and that poets are again such natural and simple figures in the popular mind as they were in other ages. They are not. There are still thousands of women and young men to whom the sibylline affectations of a Cocteau and the family charades of the Sitwells are the essential expression of what a poet's life should be. But it is possible to believe, for it is true, that the good poets of the time have ceased to accept such daguerreotypes as accurate representations of themselves. And it is possible to believe that the best of modern poetry belongs in the world we live in as no poetry has done for many, many years.

Yeats, who is the best of modern poets, may be taken in

this as the most characteristic. Not in his capacity as a man of politics or as the director of a theatre but in his capacity as poet, Yeats has refused the customary costume. He is no self-conscious genius exploiting his difference from other men — and inventing differences where none exist. He is quite simply a man who is a poet. And his poetry is no escape from time and place and life and death, but, on the contrary, the acceptance of these things and their embodiment.

How great his present stature is and how greatly we owe that present stature to the revolution in his art, any man may see by looking at the record of his work. Between the faint, vague, lovely wandering of his first romantic poems and the strong presentness, the urgent voice, of such a poem as *Byzantium*, is not only the distance between mediocrity and greatness but the distance also between a poet of private speech and the satin salons and a poet of public speech and the world. Yeats's later poetry is poetry of the world. It is the first English poetry in a century which has dared to re-enter the world. It is the first poetry in English in more than a century in which the poem is again an act upon the world. It is the first poetry in generations which can cast a shadow in the sun of actual things — men's lives, men's wills, men's future. With Yeats, poetry becomes an engine capable of employing all the mind, all the knowledge, all the strength. With Yeats, poetry ceases to be a closet avocation to the practice of which a man could bring only nostalgia, only melancholy, only fantasy, only arts and doubtings of escape. Writing as Yeats writes, a man need not pretend an ignorance of the world, need not affect a strangeness from his time, need not go mooning through an endless attic with the starlight clicking on the roof.

The later poetry of Yeats is, then, the measure of the actual achievement of the poetic revolution associated with his name. It is not, however, the measure of the ultimate importance of that achievement. And not only because no one can yet foresee what the ultimate influence of the poetic revolution may be, but for a better reason. The later poetry of Yeats, because of Yeats's somewhat isolated situation in Ireland and because of Yeats's age, has not been called upon to employ the results of the poetic revolution at the point where those results may prove to be most useful. Yeats has moved only briefly and unwillingly at the point where the poetic revolution crosses the revolution in the social and political and economic structure of the post-war world, which so deeply concerns our generation in this country. But it is precisely at that point that the greatest victories of modern poetry may be won.

History is supposed, by the economic determinists, to proceed without the cheap and vulgar aid of coincidence. It is very hard, nevertheless, to explain otherwise than by coincidence the fact that the revolution in the art of poetry which enabled poetry to re-enter the actual world, took place ten years or so before the social and economic and political revolution which today requires poetry either to re-enter the actual world or to perform a final bloodless suicide upon its laurel mountain. Thomas Mann, who has reason to know, says of the nature of our time that in our time the destiny of man presents its meanings in political terms. A political world and a destiny presented in political terms are a world and a destiny with which nineteenth-century poetry is impotent to deal. They are perhaps the world and the destiny to which modern poetry is best adapted.

The truth of the first of these two statements is visible

enough. The poets of our time to whom the revolution in poetry was unreal, or who were unable for one reason or another to profit by it, have found themselves face to face with a brutal choice — to resign either from their age or from their art. Many of them, unable to comprehend within a rhetorical art a generation of violence and tragedy and menace, have been driven either out of their art into silence or out of their age into dreams.

The truth of the second statement is still to be established by such obvious evidence. Younger poets of our generation who have known how to profit by the example of Pound and of Pound's generation *have* been able to use the revolution in their art to meet the revolution of their age. But so far their achievements are tentative, and their accomplishment is not so much an arrival as a transition. It is, furthermore, a transition which has been very little acknowledged. The critics have for the most part discussed it, when they have discussed it at all, under some variant of the claptrap phrase Art and Propaganda — as though nothing more important were under discussion than a voluntary selection of subject matter — as though men faced with the desperate necessity of bringing their art to terms with their time were concerned with nothing more important than the question whether to write of riots or of roses.

But tentative though it may now be, it is, nevertheless, probable that this transition toward a poetry capable of accepting a political and revolutionary era upon its own terms is a transition capable, if effected, of reaching the greatest and most noble ends — the true ends of poetry — the ends of all the greatest poetry of the past. It is a transition capable of restoring a poetry of public speech.

It is a transition *capable* of that end. Whether or not it

will actually achieve that end is another question. At the present moment, the transition is dangerously threatened from within by those who should be most responsible for its success. Certain of the young English poets, directly engaged in dealing with the revolution of their age, and consciously employing the methods of the revolution in their art, seem for some inexplicable reason to be doubling on their tracks. Or more exactly they seem to be engaged in pushing the use of idioms of living speech inherited from their predecessors on beyond the true limits of those idioms into the artificiality of a new closet poetry. Instead of the live phrases of passionate utterance to be found in Yeats — the human rhythms, the beautiful simplicities of which the beauty is most apparent because it was always there but never till this moment seen — instead of all this, there is an inversion of naturalness which uses natural utterance for satiric and subjective ends. Auden and his imitators have chosen for their poetic language the living language of the time, but the living language in its most banal and deadened phrases. They have created from this stereotyped language a satiric, and sometimes a lyric, poetry of great power. But the meanings of this poetry are not outward toward the world but inward toward the private references of the poet.

The transition, therefore, may not ever be fulfilled. It may never move beyond its present tentative and incomplete position. But it is, nevertheless, a phenomenon of great interest and concern to all who occupy themselves with poetry. For it is a progress in the one direction in which poetry can possibly proceed if poetry is to become again the thing it has been at its greatest reach.

Autumn, 1938.

QUESTION OF AUDIENCE

TWO nights ago I read in the paper that *Waiting For Lefty* was to close. I went to see it again. It was a sweltering night — air you could hardly breathe outside and inside a slow, sweating breathlessness. There were no more than half a dozen theatres open in the city and those few barely filled. Even the gentlemen who live by having (and publishing) one dramatic reaction regularly every day like bran flakes for breakfast had given up: they were filling their news columns with personal items about parties in Hollywood. The theatre was dead — the theatre as Broadway and Broadway's intellectuals understand the word. There wasn't enough life in it to justify the ads.

That was outside the Longacre. Inside the Longacre it was also hot. Every time the curtain went down the temperature of the room went up. There was no more breeze than a hat would make hanging in a closet. But no one, after the first minute, noticed. Because inside the Longacre something was going on which made heat and air and almost everything else irrelevant. You can call it anything you like. If the word *theatre* means the kind of thing the Pulitzer Prize judges recognize and the kind of thing the critics of the one-a-day approve then it wasn't theatre. But if it wasn't then so much the worse for the word. And so much the worse for those who use it.

Now the point I am trying to make is not that Clifford Odets is a good playwright nor that his work is better than anything else in New York. The first fact is pretty widely known and the second is obvious. The point I am trying to make is that Clifford Odets and the Group and a crowded sweltering audience created among them something moving and actual and alive. And the implication I am trying to suggest is that this moving, actual, living thing existed only in the Longacre theatre and not in the theatres where the regular seasonal offerings familiar to the trade were wheeling through their mannequin ceremonies.

In that point and in that implication lies a truth which American writers, revolutionary or not, cannot continue to ignore. The truth is this: The American theatre is dead and the American theatre is now alive. The American theatre is as dead as we have been saying it was for many years and the American theatre is more alive than it has ever been in its history. What is dead is the commercial theatre with all its appurtenances, all its critical and promotional paraphernalia, all its tricks, all its grimaces. What is alive is the workers' theatre with all its lacks, all its poverty, all its meagerness — and all its passion, its eloquence, its insolence, its force. The workers' theatres offer a stage and a hearing for the best work and the most honest work any writer of verse or prose is capable of doing. For the first time since I have known anything about such matters there exists a theatre in which dishonesty is not demanded, in which hokum is not a compulsory ingredient. There is offered, in other words, a theatre for art.

And there is offered also something more. There is offered an opportunity to affect the life of our time. No serious artist, no matter what he might pretend — no matter what the conditions of importance of his life might force him to pretend — has ever doubted that his art would have fundamental meaning for him only when he could feel the impact of his art not upon the appreciation of an audience, not upon the judgment of a critic, but upon the life of the generation of which he is a part. There is no greater persuader than art when it is permitted to touch the vital nerves. There is nothing more frivolous than art when it is denied access to the sources of life. In the workers' theatres art may touch and reach. It may be more powerful than the possessors of power, more serious than the creators of knowledge, more persuasive than the actions of armies.

Now, sooner or later, it is probable that the people of this country will be faced with a choice of which one alternative will be fascism. The appeal of fascism, since it has no intellectual content and no economic logic, is purely emotional. Against emotion only emotion, in the great masses of men, can fight. Against the false and journalistic emotions of fascism the real and human emotions of art must contend. There therefore exists in the workers' theatres not only an opportunity for an honest art and not only an opportunity for the impact of an honest art upon the life of this generation but an opportunity for the delivery of that impact at the precise point where it is most essential that the life of this generation should be influenced. In support of fascism, when the time comes, there will be enlisted all the forces which fascism can buy — the press, the movies, the commercial theatre. They will be lined up as they were lined up during the war. Their power will be overwhelming. Against them will stand the artists whom money cannot buy. And yet, and despite the discrepancy in numbers, in wealth, in everything else which creates discrepancies, the conflict will not be unequal. No power on earth can outpersuade the great and greatly felt work of art when its purpose is clear and its creator confident.

August, 1935.

A STAGE FOR POETRY

ONE year the intelligent thing to say is that the American theatre needs poetry. The next the appropriate thing to say is that the American theatre has been given poetry. Neither observation seems to me to make sense. I understand the literal meaning of the words. And I understand more or less what they intend to say. People who argue in one year that the American theatre needs poetry mean that the language of the commercial stage is barren — which indeed it is and will continue to be. And people who later rejoice that the American theatre has been given what it needs have reference to the fact that a number of revivals, Shakespearean or other, are in process or in prospect. But even so the sense of the remarks escapes me. I am unable to understand how a theatre can 'need' poetry, and I am totally incapable of comprehending how, even if the need could exist, a Shakespearean revival or even ten Shakespearean revivals could satisfy it.

Poetry is not one of the things which a man or an institution can need or not need, as a shave or a new drop curtain might be needed or not needed. It is one of the things which happen and which, happening, leave nothing as it was before. You might as well say that a picture needed painting as to say that a theatre needed poetry: until the picture *is* painted there is no possibility of knowing whether it needs painting or not, or whether, painted, it would be acceptable or even endurable. As for the Shakespearean revivals — the acting of superb verse plays written in England three hundred years ago may be a source of the greatest gratification to American audiences but it puts no poetry into the manuscripts of American playwrights. Accurately speaking, it does nothing to the American theatre at all.

The American theatre is not what American audiences see but what American writers write, and though there is no reason on earth why American audiences should confine themselves to American writers, there is every reason why the term 'American Theatre' should be used with precision. We have an ancient and provincial habit in this country of congratulating ourselves on our intelligence and good taste in borrowing from abroad, and occasionally we even go so far as to indulge ourselves in the pleasant pretense that what we borrow we own. The assumption that we have a rich musical culture because we hear Toscanini conduct Mozart is a case in point. But the attitude is more general than that. It rests upon one of the fundamental articles of our national credo. What we really believe in in America is not art but culture.

If you believe in art the artist is important. If you believe in culture the audience is important. We were picture collectors before we painted pictures. We were collectors of architecture before we had an architecture of our own. And we were theatregoers before we had a theatre. We are still theatregoers. We criticize plays as theatregoers: our dramatic critics are, for the most part, merely more regular first-nighters. We write plays as theatregoers: our really successful playwrights owe their success to their understanding, not of the human, but of the public, heart.

And we enjoy in consequence a theatregoer's theatre — a theatre in which entertainment is the real criterion and such esthetic standards as there are, are cultural. A theatregoer's theatre may be saved from prosiness by Shakespearean revivals. But the American theatre cannot be. The American theatre, if it is to be saved at all, must save itself.

And the real question is not whether it should, but whether it will. That is to say the real question is not whether the American theatre *needs* poetry. The real question is whether poetry will be provided. The distinction is not capricious. It rests upon certain substantial considerations as to the nature of poetry which most people who think and write about the matter in this connection tend to forget. The lady who pounds indignantly out of a Broadway theatre snorting that the theatre needs poetry is pretty apt to be the kind of lady who has never considered very attentively what poetry is. She will belong, nine times out of ten, to that popular school of American thought which conceives of a poem as an embellished bit of prose — a more decorative and ornamental and uplifting and tear-producing bit of prose. Indeed she will belong to that school ten times out of ten, because it is only if you think of poetry as decoration, as something added to or superimposed upon ordinary language as one would add silk curtains to a bedroom for romance, that it is possible to talk about the theatre's 'need for poetry' at all. The idea is that thin, sleazy language becomes poetry if you varnish it with high-sounding phrases. The idea, specifically, is that the orotund and affected rhetoric with which recent Irish playwrights have captivated the suburban ladies of New York is poetry. And that the theatre needs more of it.

The only trouble with this theory is that it isn't so. Nothing in heaven or under it has less to do with embellishment or decoration than poetry. Nothing in Ireland is less like rhetoric than the true and precise poetry of Yeats. Poetry is not a decorated prose, but a stripped and vivid speech which owes its power not to veneers of ornament but to nakedness of saying. Poets have written in rococo, but they are not greater but less great because they have. It is the sole Arabian tree and not the rich jewel in the Ethiope's ear which makes Shakespeare. The supreme metaphor of European poetry has, for all its paraphernalia, a nearsighted tailor peering in the evening light.

All of which comes down to saying that the writing of poetry is not the patterning and heightening of prose, but a revolutionary and entire invention. And that the writing of poetry for the stage is not a matter of heightening the language of the existing stage, but of reinventing the theatre from the inside out. You cannot call a poet in and say: 'Here is a play. The language is barren. Enrich it!' You can only say: 'Here is the stage. Can you discover a use for it?'

To professionals of the theatre that second question must sound fantastically ridiculous or ridiculously arrogant. To anyone concerned with the life of poetry in our time it has a very different sound. It makes explicit and formidable the challenge to that art. Poetry cannot continue in its present state; if it attempts to do so it will die and the obsequies will pass unnoticed. An art which lives by the production of little books to lie on little tables; an art which must be cherished by foundations and female societies and literary prizes; an art which is appreciated only by the peculiarly sensitive or the delicately lonely or the deeply passionate, is not an art in flower. To flourish, an art must touch the general mind of its time — not merely the most sensitive minds of its time. Poetry has lost that touch. It has lost it at both ends of the process of communication. Its roots are in a potted earth which men find increasingly sterile and waterless as this civilization grows older. And its blossoming is in a hothouse.

The suffocation at the root can be and will be cured by the cracking of the pot. There are signs already that fissures have occurred; that the filaments which sustain the art are working down again into the life, not of the fashionable world, not of the colleges, not of the literature business, but of living men. The only question now is whether the contact with vitality can be restored without the smashing of the whole container and the substitution of a better. But even if poetry succeeds in finding an earth which can sustain and feed it, it will still be dwarfed and choked unless it can branch into open sun and air. And there the theatre alone can help it. Only by the invention of a poetic theatre at once popular and true can the art of poetry recover its stature.

It is because this problem is so pressing, and because so much depends upon the outcome, that the various experiments already made here and abroad are important. Most of them have been made by poets having very little knowledge of the theatre. T. S. Eliot's play of Thomas à Becket and W. H. Auden's *Dance of Death* are well-known instances. One, Maxwell Anderson's *Winterset*, has been made by a playwright with the contrary qualifications. From the point of view of those interested in the reform of the existing stage, the Anderson play is much the most interesting of the three named. From the point of view of those interested in poetry and a poetic drama, it is much the least. But even to these latter *Winterset* has a great deal to say. Mr. Anderson, with unusual courage, has left his easy, unimportant historical romances behind him and turned to the life and mentality of his own time. He has faced some of the difficulties inherent in the effort to present that life and mentality in verse. And the result is a play which cannot help being technically useful and substantially encouraging to other writers.

But in spite of that achievement the question still remains. What use can poetry make of the stage? Specifically, what use can modern poetry make of the modern stage? What can be retained? What must be destroyed? One certainty is that a true poetic theatre would be more realistic than the existing stage: not less. The much-discussed realism of the existing stage is not actually real at all. On the contrary it is an imitation of reality — a factually accurate imitation of the familiar surface of day-to-day life by which we are all, in all our experiences, cheated and fooled. The sets are the known habitual rooms in which the deceptions of our daily lives take place. The faces are the deceiving faces. The underlying reality, which all but the most cynical of us must believe to exist behind these surfaces, is nowhere divulged and nowhere made visible. The outsides of our lives are reproduced with the most faithful and meaningless veracity. But nowhere are we shown the naked flesh. At the most there is an arrangement, a patterning, of these external appearances which goes by the name of plot; or a pinching and pulling of these faces which goes by the name of character development; or a clever and superficial comment upon these surfaces which goes by the name of insight. Even the occasional perceptions of a dramatist of the stature of O'Neill are merely explanations delivered from the outside like the comments of an ingenious and understanding friend. For the rest there is the dazzle of the school of Shaw — dazzle like the shine reflected from a window through which no one sees.

Never on the existing stage, as it did on the Greek stage, does the play *happen*. Never is it anything more than a description. The very realism of the existing stage stands in the way, for this realism is the realism of description — detailed, precise, and painstaking, but description nevertheless. It is for this reason that a true poetic theatre would be more actual, more real, than the theatre we have. For the art of poetry, despite all its loving traducers and despite all its vulgar defenders, is not the art of valentine-making. Poetry is not ornament, is not flowers, is not the pumping up of language with metaphors, is not a lovely embroidered cover drawn across a dirty fact, is not beguiling and pleasure-giving fancy, is not a charm to make the mind forget, is not a paint, an enamel, a veneer. Poetry — and I mean by poetry the thing itself as one or two men living write it — is revelation, is discovery. Its essence is precision, but precision of the emotions, not the mind. Its quality is to illuminate from within, not to describe from without. Its language is not communication, but experience.

If ever a true poetic play is written for the modern stage, it will make palpable and real what has never been real, what has never been palpable, in our time. That it may also, in the process, destroy the modern stage is a possibility which those who talk so pleasantly of the theatre's need for poetry will do well to consider.

November, 1935.

POETRY AND THE PUBLIC
WORLD

THERE is a very good reason why the relation of poetry to political revolution should interest our generation. Poetry, to most people, stands for the intensely personal life of the individual spirit. Political revolution stands for the intensely public life of a society with which the individual spirit must, but must not, make its peace. The relation between the two implies a conflict our generation understands — the conflict between the personal life of one man and the impersonal life of many men.

But there is no very good reason why our generation should interest itself in the talk about this conflict which now fills the literary journals. The believers in many men say that poetry should be part of political revolution. The believers in one man say that poetry should have no truck with political revolution. Neither position is interesting. The real question is not whether poetry *should* have to do with political revolution or whether it shouldn't. The real question is whether poetry is of such a nature, and political revolution of such a nature, that poetry *can* have to do with political revolution. For it may be said that poetry *should* do this, or should not do that, only when it is meant that poetry *can* do this or cannot do that: poetry has no other laws than the laws of its own nature.

The only intelligent discussion of the question, therefore, is a discussion in terms of poetry, and of the nature
of poetry. It is a discussion which should begin by asking
what the nature of poetry is, and specifically whether
poetry is, by its nature, an art or whether it is of some
other nature. For if poetry is an art, then poetry can do
whatever an art can do. But if poetry is not an art, then
the limitations of poetry are of a different kind.

Much has been written on that subject and much said
by men of many generations who have published books
or talked in evenings or on roads walking or at other
times. There are those on the one hand who say that
poetry cannot be an art because it is something more than
an art, being a kind of revelation of Truth or Beauty or
Goodness. To these people it is clear that poetry can have
no relation to political revolution, because political revolution is outside in the air and sky and not inside in the
spirit where poetry can reveal it. There are those on the
other hand who say that poetry cannot be an art because
poetry is something less than an art, being nothing but
another way of writing what can also be written in prose.
To these people also poetry can have nothing to say about
political revolution, because prose can say it better. There
are, finally, those who say that poetry is neither something
more than an art nor something less than an art, but
simply an art. To these last, poetry has to do with political
revolution if art has to do with political revolution: otherwise not.

But though there are three possible opinions, and though
all three of these opinions are held by numerous and re-
spectable people, all three are not of equal value. The
opinion, for example, that poetry is something more than
an art is an opinion widely taught in schools and broadly

held among English-speaking people. But it is an opinion difficult for readers of poetry to credit, for it leads to definitions like the definition offered recently by an English poetess, that a poem is 'an uncovering of truth of so fundamental and general a kind that no other name besides poetry is adequate except truth.' Poetry, in other words, is not the poem itself, but some content the poem makes available, as a bank check makes available a sum of money. It is a truth which the poem reveals as the boy in the fairy story discovered the giant's heart in the duck's egg in the church well on the lake isle. The trouble with this definition of poetry is that it applies to certain poems only. There are poems in which 'an uncovering of truth' occurs. Some of them are good poems. Many of them are written by women. But not all poems are of this kind. In Homer, for example, there is not only 'an uncovering of truth': there are also descriptions of the shapes of men and animals and the color of water and the revengefulness of gods. And the greatest poems in all languages are remembered not for their messages but for themselves.

In the same way the opinion that poetry is something less than an art, being no more than a sort of conventionalized prose, is difficult to accept. Those who hold to this opinion believe that poetry is not different in kind from prose, but different only in verbal form: it is merely another way of saying the same thing. Thus there are old poets who say to young poets: 'Never write in verse what you could write in prose.' There are teachers who say to students: 'This is prose because it is not poetry.' There are critics who say to readers: 'Poetry is dead. Prose is driving it out of our modern world.'

To say any of these things you must, of course, believe that poetry is merely another way of saying what prose can also say, a competing way of writing. You can only talk about prose driving poetry out of our modern world if you think of prose and poetry as competing ways of writing. You can only talk about not writing in verse what you could write in prose if you think of verse and prose as alternative methods of accomplishing the same thing. But anyone who has ever written them knows of his own knowledge that prose and poetry are not merely alternative ways of saying the same thing, but that they are different ways of saying different things. What can be said in one cannot be said in the other. The attempt to undo a poem into prose leaves nothing but a little silly heap of words like the dust into which the antiquities of tombs disintegrate at the touch of air. A poem is not *a* way in which something may be written, but *the* way in which something may be written. And the thing which may be written in this way is the poem.

It seems likely, therefore, that those people are right who believe that poetry is neither more than an art nor less than an art, but an art only, and that the relation between poetry and political revolution is a relation to be discussed in these terms. But in terms of art it is difficult to agree that poetry is of such a nature, and political revolution of such a nature, that poetry can have no truck with political revolution.

Art is a method of dealing with our experience of this world, which makes that experience, *as* experience, recognizable to the spirit. There are other methods of dealing with our experience of this earth which translate it into intellectual terms or extract from it moral meanings. Art is not such a method. Art is not a technique for extracting truths, nor a system of signals for communicating explanations. Art is not a diver's glass for seeing inward, nor a mathematic for arriving at an ultimate understanding of our lives. Art is an organization of experience in terms of experience, the purpose of which is the recognition of experience. It is an interpreter between ourselves and that which has happened to us, the purpose of which is to make legible what it is that has happened. It is an organization of water in terms of water, an organization of faces in terms of faces, an organization of streetcars and vermilion and death in terms of streetcars and vermilion and death. It is an organization of experience comprehensible not in terms of something else, but of itself; not in terms of significance, but of itself; not in terms of truth even, but of itself. The truth of a work of art is the truth of its organization. It has no other truth.

Art, therefore, is not selective. It is catholic. There are not certain experiences which are fit for art and certain other experiences which are not fit for art. Any experience, whether of violence or of contemplation or of sensuality or of wonder or of disgust, of which the spirit demands recognition may be brought to the labor of art. And if this is true of all art it is true also of that form of art which is poetry. There are not certain *kinds* of experience which are proper for poetry; nor, conversely, are the experiences which poetry makes recognizable experiences peculiar to poetry alone. The experience which poetry makes recognizable may be the experience *of* anything. It may be, as it has most frequently been in the practice of the art, the experience of love or of the idea of God or of death or of the beauty — the always and in each new generation newly astonishing beauty — of this world. But it may also be, as it has often been, a very different experience. It may be any experience whatever which requires for its intensity the intensity of the poetic line, the shock of the poetic association, the compression of the poetic statement, the incantation of the poetic word. It may be any experience of which the intensity is so great that only a corresponding intensity of order can give it shape, as the tension of flight gives form and beauty to the beating of wings.

Poetry is to violent emotion what the crystal is to the condensing salt or the equation to laborious thinking — release, identity, and rest. What words cannot do as words because they can only speak, what rhythm and sound cannot do as rhythm and sound because they have no speech, poetry can do because its sound and its speech are a single incantation. Only poetry can produce that absorption of the reasoning mind, that release of the listening nature, that solution of the deflections and distractions of the surfaces of sense, by which intense experience is admitted, recognized, and known. Only poetry can present the closest and therefore least visible experiences of men in such form that they, reading, may say: 'Yes ... Yes ... It is like that. . . . That is what it is truly like.'

II

There is therefore, if poetry is an art, no religious rule, no critical dogma, which excludes from poetry the political experience of men. There is only a question. Is the political experience of our time an experience which requires, for its intensity the intensity of poetry? Is the political experience of our time an experience personal and immediate and intense as are the experiences to which poetry, and poetry alone, can give shape and order and recognition?

Certainly there was a time in the lives of those of us who are now no longer young when political experience was neither close nor personal nor in any meaning of the word intense. Political experience in the years before the war was external experience which made no part of the personal lives of men but was rather like a game or diversion or contest. A man lived in his house and his street and his friends, and politics were elsewhere. The public world was the public world and the private world was the private world. Poetry in that time concerned itself with the private world. When it dealt with the public world it dealt with it in private terms, presenting, for example, the public problem of the state in terms of the private mystery of kingship. Either that or it surrendered its rights as poetry and entered the political service of the government as did Kipling and the poets of the British Empire School.

But because it was true thirty years ago that the public world was the public world and the private world the private world, and because it was true thirty years ago that poetry in its quality of poetry had very little traffic with the public world, it does not follow that either is true today. Indeed the evidence not only of our own eyes but of those who speak to us with authority tells us that what was true thirty years ago is now not true but the contrary of the truth. Thomas Mann says to us that whereas twenty years ago, at the time when he wrote his *Reflections of an Unpolitical Man*, he opposed political activity with all his power in the name of freedom and culture, he has now come to see 'that the German bourgeoisie had erred in thinking that a man of culture could remain unpolitical ... that the political and the social are parts of the human: they belong to the totality of human problems and must be drawn into the whole.' We, too, have begun to see this. We, too, have begun to know that the public world is no longer on one side and the private world on the other.

Indeed the public world with us has *become* the private world, and the private world has become the public. We see our private individual lives in terms of the public and numerous lives of those who live beside us, and we see the lives of those who live beside us in terms of the lives we thought once were our own. We live, that is to say, in a revolutionary time in which the public life has washed in over the dikes of private existence as sea water breaks over into the fresh pools in the spring tides till everything is salt. The world of private experience has become the world of crowds and streets and towns and armies and mobs. The world of many men equaling man, of every man equaling men, has taken the place of the world of the lonely walker, the self-searcher, the single figure staring by night into mirrors, into stars. The single individual, whether he so wishes or not, has become a part of a world which contains also Austria and Czechoslovakia and China and Spain. The victories of tyrants and the resistance of peoples halfway round the world are as near to him as the ticking of the clock on the mantel. What happens in his morning paper happens in his blood all day, and Madrid, Nanking, Prague, are names as close to him as the names by which he counts his dearest losses.

This we know to be true of our own knowledge. And since we know it to be true, we know also the answer to the question we have asked. If our life as members of society, which is to say our public life, which is to say our political life, has become a life which moves us to personal indignation, which fills us with personal fear, which suggests to us also private hopes, we have no choice but to say that our experiences of this life are experiences of intense and personal emotion. And if our experiences of this life are experiences of intense and personal emotion, then they are such experiences as poetry can make recognizable — such experiences as perhaps poetry alone can make recognizable.

But if we know this to be true, then the whole question of the relation of poetry to political revolution is a different question from the question commonly discussed. The real wonder is not the wonder which the literary dilettantes say they feel — the wonder that poetry should deal so much with a public world which concerns it so little. The real wonder is that poetry should deal so little with a public world which concerns it so much. What requires explanation is not the fact that a few contemporary poets have attempted to give poetic order to the political experience of our time, but the fact that no contemporary poet has yet succeeded in that effort — the fact that no contemporary poet has yet presented to us, in the personal and yet universal terms of poetry, our generation's experience of the political world. Some of the greatest — Yeats most notably — have touched it. But not even Yeats has presented the contemporary experience of the political world *as* experience, in terms of experience — so related, in such words, with such implications both of meaning and of sense, that we have recognized it for what it is. Not even Yeats has done what poetry must do; what poetry has, in other periods, done.

In a valuable paper on 'Hamlet and the Nature of Reality,' Professor Theodore Spencer of Harvard has shown how the greatest of English poets reduced to poetic order and made recognizable the common experience of his age. He has shown how the conflict of appearance and reality which gives *Hamlet* its dramatic tension relates to the conflict of appearance and reality characteristic of the thinking of the time: the conflict between accepted

Ptolemaic notions of cosmology on the one hand and
Copernican ideas of the universe upon the other; between
orthodox Aristotelian conceptions of the morality of rulers
and Machiavelli's theories of 'realistic' government; between Renaissance beliefs as to the position of man in
nature and Montaigne's views as to man's total dependence upon the divine grace. Shakespeare's play is such an
organization of the moral confusion and intellectual anxi-
ety of his contemporaries as a great poet can accomplish,
and Hamlet remains to our day the one figure in which
we recognize the experience of intellectual doubt at that
extremest point where doubt is no longer possible and only
belief can be supported. His words are the words in which
we still speak to ourselves of the pain of believing that the
true appearance may be only the apparent truth.

What is really remarkable about the experience of our
generation is the fact that no comparable organization of
the public yet private life of our time has been attempted
by contemporary poetry. It is this fact, and not the fear
that poetry may be misused for political purposes, which
should trouble the lovers of poetry. They will not dispose
of it by explaining mockingly that such a task requires a
Shakespeare and that contemporary poetry has produced
no Shakespeare.

It is true that the labor is difficult. Difficult at all times,
the labor of poetic organization becomes almost unbear-
ably difficult when the appearance to be mastered is an
appearance private in its nearness, public in its form.
Poetry, however some of its practitioners may talk of it,
is not a magical art, and poets, like others, must understand before they can create understanding. They must
themselves see the shape and meaning of experience before
they can give it shape and meaning. And there are few

among us of any occupation who know the shape and meaning of the time in which we live. The difference between the chaos of unordered perceptions and the order of the poetic perception is the difference of the poetic act; and the poetic act, however swift, however easy, however genial it may seem, is an act as laborious as any accomplished by men, for it is an act in which there are no aids, no tools, no implements, no mathematics, no sextants — an act in which one man alone struggles with an appearance which will not show its true and actual face until he forces it. The Greek myth of Proteus is the true myth of this labor. The poet's struggle is to constrain the live thing in the net to leave its changing forms and take its actual form, which is the god's form, and be known.

> The pelt falls from him and the sea cow's shape,
> The fish's scarlet, the shark's wrinkled skin,
> The seal's eyes and the brine-encircled nape,
> The foam's evasion, the down-diving fin —
> All cheats and falsehoods of his vain escape:
> Changed to himself, sea-sleeked and dripping yet,
> The god lies caught and naked in the taking net.

But though it is certain that the struggle to compel the false appearance to be true is peculiarly difficult in a time like ours, when the god to be forced is a god we have never seen and even the appearances are appearances with which we are unfamiliar, it is not the difficulty alone which stands in the way. Labor as difficult has been done before this, and not by Shakespeare only. The characteristic achievements of poetry are not reserved for the greatest poets alone, but appear also in the work of lesser men.

III

The true explanation of the failure of contemporary poetry to bring to poetic recognition the experience of our

time is the nature of the influences which continue to dom-
inate that poetry and the character of the models on which
it is formed. More precisely, it is the fact that the poetry
we call contemporary — the poetry, that is to say, to
which we apply the word 'modern' — is not actually contemporary or modern, but belongs to a time earlier than
our own and was formed by necessities which are not ours.
It is a poetry which belongs, in its French originals, to
Verlaine and Laforgue and the last decades of the last century; in its English derivations, to T. S. Eliot and Ezra
Pound and the first two decades of this. It is a poetry
formed not by the human and political necessities of our
own world but by the literary necessities of the world before the war.

The poetry we call contemporary was originally, and
still remains, a poetry of literary revolt. As such it is a
poetry adapted not to the creation of new poetic organizations of experience, but to the destruction of old poetic
organizations. As the common experience of men changes
from one generation to the next, the organizations of experience in poetry must change also. But the new organizations are never new beginnings, new constructions, but
always reconstructions. The physical materials of which
they are made — the words, the accents of the words, the
sounds of the words, the meaning, the syntax — have all
been used before: they have all been built into work now
standing. Before they can be used for new work they must
first be knocked free of the old mortar, pried loose from
the old nails. It is for this reason that the revolutions in
poetry, as in other arts, are necessary and must take place.
Whenever the experience of a new generation differs so
widely from the experience of the previous generation that
the organizations of experience which were previously use-

ful are no longer useful, whenever a truly different organization of experience is demanded, the old organizations must first be dismantled and taken down.

'Modern' poetry in English, like its French *Symboliste* prototype, is poetry of this kind. The French poets called *Symbolistes* had one thing in common and only one — a common hatred of the formal and rhetorical poetry of Parnasse '*avec sa perfection technique, ses vers sculpturaux, ses rimes opulentes, son archéologie hellénique, romaine et hindou.*' Their common purpose was, as Verlaine put it, to '*tordre le cou à l'Eloquence.*'

Pound, the first of the American poets justly called 'modern,' was also a hater of rhetoric and a twister of tails. Pound was the great dismantler, the great wrecker of brownstone fronts, the great tearer down of imitation French châteaux and imitation Gothic railroad stations. He was a wrecker to whom not merely the politely dead poetry of the generation immediately prior to his own, but the whole world which accepted that poetry, was an obsolescence, a solecism calling for the crowbar and the sledge. He was a dynamiter who hated not only the Georgian Anthology and the overstuffed verse of the years before the war, but the whole Edwardian organization of experience out of which all the experience and most of the poetry had long since leaked like the horsehair out of an old family sofa, leaving nothing but a stiff brittle shape which dogs avoided and even lovers would not use. He was, as he himself said of Laforgue, an exquisite poet, a deliverer of the nations, a Numa Pompilius, a father of light. His dreams at night were of words chipped clean of the rhetoric which staled them, words planed clean of the literary varnish which had tinted them to golden oak, words scraped back to the white pine with the white pine odor. He was, and he still is, one of the great clearers and cleansers of cluttered earth. If a new generation does not see him in these terms it is because a new generation does not know the architecture he has overthrown. These poems which are wall ornaments now that the old buildings have gone down were tools once — hooked iron crowbars and mallet-headed sledges and cold steel chisels of destruction.

Eliot also, who will perhaps be remembered for other reasons, was a wrecker of poetic forms at the time when he was writing the poems which have so influenced this generation. More effectively even than Pound, Eliot was then engaged in breaking down the existing combinations, the 'poetic' associations of words and images and sounds. He heaved the present-tense, commonplace modern world, with its suburban boredom, its Sunday-afternoon hopelessness, its park-bench despair, through the glass windows of academic poetry as Pound was never able to heave it. He was more destructive than Pound because he cared more than Pound; he had lived in the house himself. Eliot in his heart loved the academic traditions he attacked, and he did what he did in bitterness and a curious inward-turning revenge rather than in hope of a better poetry to follow. He worked, not as Pound did, to clear the earth and air for a different structure, but in a kind of passionate disgust with himself and his time, hating the necessity of destruction and destroying only to make its hatefulness more plain. The fact that it was his own time he hated, and not the poetic past with which his own time was at war, gives his work the cold, premeditated violence of the suicide.

Modern poetry is the poetry of these masters, and of the war and pre-war generations which formed them. It was, in its own time, a needed and cleansing poetry of literary revolt. But it was never a poetry capable of the new labor of construction which must now be done. Revolutionists are rarely successful rebuilders of the worlds they have brought down, and the continuation of the pretense of revolution beyond the victory of revolution produces a peculiar frustration and sterility with which we in our time are only too familiar. Contemporary poetry is in large part such a continuation of pretended revolution. The early attitudes and idioms of Eliot are imitated long after their relevance has vanished, not because a new relevance has been found for them, but because their flavor is delightful — irony is a speech which can be bold without responsibility, and rejection is an attitude which can be wise without risk. So, too, Pound's early demands for innovation are still in fashion; not because the conditions of Pound's demands still exist, but because innovation is a delightful criterion of accomplishment — it relieves the poet of all other duty.

It is this characteristic of contemporary poetry which explains its failure to make recognizable to us our experience of our time. To write in faith and credit of such experience as ours, and to bring it to recognition, requires the responsible and dangerous language of acceptance and belief. The responsible language of acceptance and belief is not possible to the poetry of literary revolt. The Hamlet of Shakespeare was the acceptance of a difficult age and the demonstration of the place, in that age, of poetry. The Hamlet of Laforgue, and after him of Eliot and after him of the contemporary generation, is the rejection of a difficult age and a contemptuous comment upon the hope of poetry to deal with it. Not until contemporary poetry ceases to be the 'modern,' which is to say the pre-war, poetry of literary revolt, and not until contemporary poetry writes the Hamlet of Laforgue and Eliot out of its veins, will poetry occupy, and reduce to the order of recognition, the public-private world in which we live. When that happens, the true poetry of our own time will be written. There are already indications in the work of young poets, American as well as English, that the time is near.

June, 1939.

THE COMMUNISTS, THE WRITERS, AND THE SPANISH WAR

THOSE who disagree with the proposition that the spread of fascism is a matter of principal concern to writers in this country advance two main arguments. The first is the argument that concern with the spread of fascism, and the making of common defensive front against it, amount in effect to the fomenting of war — and not only to the fomenting of war but to the fomenting of another war horribly like the last war, another war to make the world safe for democracy. The second is the argument that the fascist issue is in actual fact nothing but a private squabble between fascism and communism,[1] of no concern to anyone but the partisans, and of ulterior and purely factional concern even to them.

This second argument is so manifestly and demonstrably unsound that it may be left to answer itself. It is the familiar argument advanced by the hypocrites and the cynical and the frivolous who do not wish to understand what is happening in Spain — who do not wish to accept the responsibility of understanding — who desire to re-

[1] Written before the Communist Party changed sides and joined up with the Nazis.

main indifferent — or, worse, who desire to hide their approval of Spanish fascism under this flimsy and ridiculous pretext. It is the cheap and easy argument of those who wish not to think. What alone gives it importance is the use its proponents make of it. They use it to attack the intelligence, if not actually the integrity, of those who, not themselves communists, stand as the communists stand in active opposition to the fascist attack. They imply that those who find themselves in this position are being 'used,' and that they are dupes and stooges.

This, if you stop to consider it, is a curious suggestion to come from liberal minds — for the word liberal is still a word to use with pride. One would have thought that issues, and particularly issues of freedom and truth, were more important to the liberal mind than being seen in the right company. One would have thought that, in the face of the fighting in Spain, even the most careful liberals would consider that the issue should come first and the vanity, the self-concern, afterward. One would have thought that liberals would recognize the issue as so clearly, so inescapably their own that it would never occur to them to wonder whether in accepting it they were being 'used.' One would have thought that they would more naturally think of themselves as the *users*, as the leaders in this fight, as the responsible men. There was after all a time in this country when the liberals were capable of leading, when they were not merely capable of terror lest they should be led. There was a time when they recognized their own causes and defended them without looking around to see who else defended them and for what reasons. To my mind there is something unpleasantly squeamish and virginal about this fear of being used, this phobia of being maneuvered — something almost indecently coy. The danger of rape has always existed in this world, but only the tenderest spirits let it keep them in at night.

The truth is that no writer worthy the name ever refused to make his position clear for fear that position might be of service to others than himself. The further truth is that the man who refuses to defend his convictions for fear he may defend them in the wrong company has no convictions.

As to the first argument, the argument that those who make common front against fascism are themselves warmakers, indistinguishable from the warmakers of 1917, the answer seems to me even simpler. The answer is that it is not we who are the makers of this war. The answer is that the war is already made. It is made in Spain. And by the war I mean the war itself, the war made by fascism, the very war against which we must defend ourselves.

It is the failure to understand this obvious, this all-too-obvious fact which misleads our critics. They perceive that there is fighting in Spain. They can hardly help perceiving it. But they do not perceive the nature of that fighting. They do not understand what it is. They think of it in terms of military history. They compare it with 1914. They decide that, because there have been no declarations of war and because the nations of Europe have not yet mobilized their armies, the Spanish war cannot be the real war against fascism which is foreseen, but must be a sort of preliminary bout which can be 'kept from spreading to the continent of Europe.' They conclude that any assistance given to the people of Spain, any support in their resistance may make it impossible to confine the war to Spain, may bring on the greater war, the real war. They conclude that those who make common cause against fascism, and particularly against fascism in Spain, foment this greater war.

The weakness of this argument lies in its assumption that the pattern of 1914 fits the facts of 1937. The military vocabulary of 1914 and 1937 are not the same. In 1914 the methodical and murderous shelling of the civil population of a Spanish seacoast town by a German fleet would have been an act of war. In 1937 it is not an act of war. The Spaniards merely die, and the Germans sail away. In 1914 the massacre of the civil population of an undefended Basque village by German planes would have been an act of war. In 1937 it is not an act of war. The Basques merely lie kicking in the fields where the machine guns caught up with them, and the Germans fly away. The wars of 1937 are not fought by declarations and mobilizations. They are fought in the back streets like the assassinations of gunmen. And for an excellent reason. For they are the assassinations of gunmen.

The point is clear enough. Those who fight against fascism are not fomenting war for the simple reason that the war is already fomented. The war is already made. Not a preliminary war. Not a local conflict. *The* war; the actual war; the war between the fascist powers and the things they would destroy. Spain is no political allegory. Spain is not, as some would have us think, a dramatic spectacle in which the conflict of our times is acted out. The actors are not actors. They truly die. The cities are not stage sets. They burn with fire. The battles are not symbols of other battles to be fought elsewhere at some other time. They are the actual war itself. And in that war, that Spanish war on Spanish earth, we, writers who contend for freedom, are ourselves, and whether we so wish or not, engaged.

This is no metaphor. It is a fact simply and patently true. Others who have seen that war at first hand can say more of it than I can. But even we who have no personal knowledge of the fighting know this much: we know that the military prestige of the fascist powers (which is to say the total prestige of the fascist powers) is engaged in the Spanish war. We know that a fascist success in the Spanish war would mean a tremendous increase in that prestige and an almost certain end of democratic institutions in France, which means, in Europe. We know that a fascist failure in the Spanish war would mean a decline in that prestige and a possible collapse of fascist forms.

We know all this not only by logic, by deductions, by suppositions. We know it in fact. Evidence is before us. Already the Spanish war has basically changed, and *changed for us*, the outlook. The victory of the Spanish government before Madrid is not a symbolic victory. It is not an augury for the future. It is a present victory having definite consequences for all haters of fascism wherever they may be. It is a present victory having foreseeable consequences *for us*.

What it signifies is this: that fascism has been defeated in its dearest hopes. The fascist theory of warfare upon which all hopes of fascist aggression have been based is a theory of quick wars and overwhelming successes — a theory of conquest by sudden and unannounced attacks upon civilian populations. This theory is essential to fascist strategy because the fascist dictatorships do not dare risk long wars with their inevitable stalemates, their internal stresses, their domestic dangers. Before the siege of Madrid it was widely believed that wars could be won by ruthless aggressors in this way, and the dictators were ardent. Since Madrid it is known that wars cannot be won against a courageous population in this way, and the dictators are sullen and afraid.

But that fact, so important to the future not only of the European democracies but of our own, was not established in a laboratory. It was not demonstrated at target practice on a range. It was proved upon the bodies and against the courage of the people of Madrid. It is the people of Spain who have won already one of the great victories against fascism. How then can we, who profit by that victory, not claim the war as ours? How then can we refuse our help to those who fight our battles — to those who truly fight our battles *now* — *now*, not in some future war — *now: now* in Spain?

June 22, 1937.

THE IRRESPONSIBLES

HISTORY — if honest history continues to be written — will have one question to ask of our generation, people like ourselves. It will be asked of the books we have written, the carbon copies of our correspondence, the photographs of our faces, the minutes of our meetings in the famous rooms before the portraits of our spiritual begetters. The question will be this: Why did the scholars and the writers of our generation in this country, witnesses as they were to the destruction of writing and of scholarship in great areas of Europe and to the exile and the imprisonment and murder of men whose crime was scholarship and writing — witnesses also to the rise in their own country of the same destructive forces with the same impulses, the same motives, the same means — why did the scholars and the writers of our generation in America fail to oppose those forces while they could — while there was still time and still place to oppose them with the arms of scholarship and writing?

It is a question the historians will ask with interest — the gentle, detached, not altogether loving interest with which historians have always questioned the impotent spirits of the dead. Young men working in the paper rubbish of our lives, the old journals, the marginal notations, the printed works, will discover (or so they will think) that the scholars and the writers of our generation in this country had been warned of danger as men were rarely warned before. They will discover (or so they will think) that the common inherited culture of the West, by which alone our scholars and our writers lived, had been attacked in other countries with a stated and explicit purpose to destroy. They will discover that that purpose had been realized. They will discover that a similar purpose backed by similar forces, created by similar conditions, was forming here. And it will seem to them strange — ironical and strange — that the great mass of American scholars and American writers made no effort to defend either themselves or the world by which they lived.

They will make, of course, the necessary reservations. They will note that societies of scholars and associations of writers adopted resolutions declaring their devotion to civilization. They will note that certain young novelists and poets, the most generous and gallant of their time, unable to endure the outrage and injustice, gave up their lives as writers and enlisted in the hopeless armies to fight brutality with force. But of those who truly faced this danger not with their bodies but their minds, of those who fought the enemies of the intellect with the weapons of the intellect, devoting to that warfare all the strength, all the imagination, all the resources of courage and inventiveness, all the watchfulness by day and night, all the last reserves of hope and skill and pain which men must use whose lives and more than lives are put in danger — of those who fought this danger with the weapons by which this danger could be overcome, they will record the names of very few. And they will ask their question, Why did we, scholars and writers in America in this time, we who had been warned of our danger not only by explicit threats but by explicit action, why did we not fight this danger while the weapons we used best — the weapons of ideas and words — could still be used against it?

It is not a question for which we are altogether unprepared. We have been writing out our answer for many years now in action and inaction, in words and in silence — in learned articles in the scientific journals and in controversial articles in the general magazines, in blank faces after the passionate words, in bored eyes refusing to believe. The answer we have prepared, the answer we have written out for history to find, is the answer Leonardo is said to have given Michelangelo when Michelangelo blamed him for his indifference to the misfortunes of the Florentines. It is the answer of our kind at many other times and places. 'Indeed,' said Leonardo, 'indeed the study of beauty has occupied my whole heart.' The study of beauty, the study of history, the study of science, has occupied our whole hearts and the misfortunes of our generation are none of our concern. They are the practical and political concern of practical and political men, but the concern of the scholar, the concern of the artist, is with other, purer, more enduring things.

This is the answer we have written down for history to find. I doubt whether it will satisfy the ironic men who come to plague us on that waterfront where Teresias was made to drink the blood and answer. I think indeed it will not satisfy them. For it has not satisfied ourselves. We say with great firmness and authority, speaking by our words and by our silence, that the misfortunes of our generation are economic and political misfortunes from which the scholar can safely hold himself apart. We say this with all the authority of the political scientists of the past to whom the misfortunes of the people were always political and economic and of no concern to the poet, the pure

105

scholar, the artist intent upon his art. We say it also with
the authority of the political scientists of the present to
whom all phenomena of whatever kind are, by hypothesis,
economic and political. But though we say it we do not
believe it. For we have observed these misfortunes. They
have been acted out for us to see. And what we have seen
is this: that the misfortunes of our time are not the misfortunes the philosophers, the theorists, the political scientists have described to us. They are not the practical concern of the practical man and therefore matters of indifference to the scholar. On the contrary, it is the practical
man and the practical man alone — the man whose only
care is for his belly and his roof — who can safely be indifferent to these troubles. The things he lives by are not
menaced. And it is precisely the scholar, the poet — the
man whose care is for the structures of the intellect, the
houses of the mind — whose heart is caught. For it is the
scholar's goods which are in danger.

It is perhaps because we have seen this and yet refuse to
see it — because we know one thing and yet continue to
declare another — that our minds are so confused and our
counsels so bewildering. Nothing is more characteristic of
the intellectuals of our generation than their failure to
understand what it is that is happening to their world.
And nothing explains that failure as precisely as their un-
willingness to see what they have seen and to know what
they do truly know. They have seen the crisis of their
time — they have seen it spelled out, played out, fought
out as few observers ever before in history saw the tragedy
exposed. They know its ending. And yet they continue to
pretend that they do not know. They continue to speak of
the crisis of their time as though the war in Europe were
that crisis — and the war, they say, is no concern of theirs.

They continue to speak of the crisis as though the imperialistic maneuvers, the struggles for markets, the propaganda in the newspapers and the radio, were the crisis — and the maneuvers of imperialism, the propaganda of the press and the struggles for trade they say are no concern of theirs. And yet they know — they know very well because they have seen — that these things are not the crisis but merely its reflections in the mirrors of action. They know that behind the war, behind the diplomatic gestures, behind the black print on the page and the hysterical voices on the air there is something deeper and more dangerous — more dangerous to *them*. They know that it is a condition of men's minds which has produced these things — a condition which existed and exists, not only in Europe but in other parts of the world as well and not least in our own country. And they know that this condition of men's minds is not a practical, a political, phenomenon of no concern to the scholar and the man of thought, but something very different.

It is not, for example, a matter of purely practical and political interest that great numbers of men in various parts of the world wish passionately and even violently to give up the long labor of liberty and to surrender their wills and their bodies and even their minds to the will of a leader, so that they may achieve at least the dignity of order, at least the dignity of obedience. It is not a matter of purely practical and political significance that whole nations of men have gladly and willingly released themselves, not only from their rights as individuals, but from their responsibilities as individuals, so that they are no longer compelled to feel or to respect the individual humanity of others — or to feel or to respect the things that individual humanity has, over many centuries, created. It

is not a matter of purely practical and political importance
that governments which once, whatever they may have
practiced, protested a respect for learning and the arts,
should now permit themselves to show not only the power
but worse, far worse, the *willingness*, the *purpose*, to en-
slave both learning and the arts. It is not a matter of
purely practical and political importance that societies
which once made part of the community of Western culture should now attempt by murder and outrage and exile
to root out that culture and to replace it with private and
parochial sciences and private and parochial arts so that
frontiers are armed, for the first time in the history of the
West, not only along the rivers and the mountains and
the boundaries of nations, but across the common earth of
culture, the free land that was never fenced before.

I think no honest man will say that these are matters of
practical and political significance alone. I think any man
who considers with coolness, and without the preconceptions of the dogmas, the character of the crisis of his time
will admit, because he will have no choice but to admit,
that this crisis is in essence a cultural crisis — a revolt of
certain classes, certain conditions of men against the inherited culture of the West and against all common culture
— a revolt by no means limited to those nations alone
where it has been successful. Wars we have had before —
many wars; murder also: inquisition of scholars: torture
of askers: suppression and mutilation of truth. But in the
past these things have been done, however hypocritically,
in the name of truth, in the name of humanity — even in
the name of God. The forms of culture were preserved —
and in the preservation of a civilization as in the preservation of an art the forms are everything. What is new and
unexampled in the times we live in is *the repudiation of the*

forms. What is new is a cynical brutality which considers moral self-justification unnecessary and therefore — and this is perhaps its worst indecency — dispenses even with the filthy garment of the hypocrite. To use brutality and force, not in the name of Right nor in the name of God, but in the name of force alone, is to destroy the self-respect and therefore the dignity of the individual life without which the existence of art or learning is inconceivable. To lie, not in the name of truth, but in the name of lies, is to destroy the common basis of communication without which a common culture cannot exist and a work of learning or of art becomes unintelligible.

The truth is — the plain and simple truth of which we have so many painful evidences — that the disorder of our time, whatever else it may now be or may become, is in its essentials a revolt against the common culture of the West. For against what but the common culture did this disorder continue to struggle in Germany long after it had overthrown the former state? There was no domestic danger for it to fear. Against what but the Western respect for the dignity of the individual was aimed the long series of outrages against the Jews? The Jews were impotent when they were subjected to the worst abuses. Against what but the Western respect for the common, the nationless, creation of the artist was aimed the destruction of the work of men like Thomas Mann? Thomas Mann had already been repudiated by his people when they accepted the government of his enemies. Against what but the Western belief in the wholeness of Western civilization was aimed the assault upon a church which was no longer a danger to any ruler and the fabrication of a paganism which needed only the blond sopranos on the ends of wires to be Wagner at his worst?

Intellectuals in America and elsewhere — writers, scientists, the men of learning — have attempted to ignore these questions. They have pretended to themselves that the burning of books, the exiling of artists, the invention of mythologies were merely incidents — afterthoughts — decorations: that the true crisis was the crisis of food, the crisis of arms, the crisis created by political forces, by economic collapse — that they had, and needed have, no truck with it. They have been wrong. These things are not incidents. They are not afterthoughts. They are the essential nature of the revolution of our age. For without this attack upon the habits of the mind, the reliances of the spirit, that revolution could not, by any possibility, have succeeded.

The revolution of our age — the revolution which has finally emerged and declared itself in action — is not the great revolution of the masses of which generous men once dreamed: and which other and less generous men have now so meanly and so bloodily betrayed. The revolution of the masses was a revolution which proposed to set up one faith against another faith, one culture against another culture: a faith in man, a faith in the power of the patterns of men's lives, against a faith in institutions and in money; a culture of the people against a culture of the exploiters of the people. The revolution which has finally and successfully emerged in action has no such faith and no such culture.

It is a revolution of negatives, a revolution of the defeated, a revolution of the dispossessed, a revolution of despair. It is a revolution created out of misery by dread of yet more misery, a revolution created out of disorder by terror of disorder. It is a revolution of gangs, a revolution *against*. And the enemy it is against, the enemy it must

destroy, is the enemy which, in all times and in all civilizations, has stood against the revolutions of the gangs — the
rule of moral law, the rule of spiritual authority, the rule of
intellectual truth. To establish the negative revolutions,
the revolutions of which the only aim is power, the revolutions which have no means but force, it is necessary first to
destroy the authority of the unseen sayings of the mind.
It is necessary to destroy the things the mind has made.
Caliban in the miserable and besotted swamp is the symbol of this revolution. As long as the unseen beauty in the
air retains its voices and its seductive music and its sting-
ing whips, the revolutions of the gangs are clumsy, blunder-
ing, grotesque, and foolish. They can bellow and threaten
and boast and gesture with their arms, but in the end the
invisible voices of the air, the invisible power of the ideal
will master them. They have one hope of success and only
one — the destruction of the whole system of ideas, the
whole respect for truth, the whole authority of excellence
which places law above force, beauty above cruelty, singleness above numbers.

It is the distinction of our time — perhaps unhappily its
most memorable distinction — that it and it alone has
provided the formula by which this overthrow could be
achieved. Only in our time has the revolution of the
gangs discovered a strategy and a leadership brutal
enough, cynical enough, cunning enough to destroy the
entire authority of the inherited culture and thereafter
to seal the doors against the searching and the asking of
the scholar's mind, the artist's mind, so that the revolution of force, the revolution of despair could flower and
fulfill its possibilities. Only in our time has the revolution of the gangs shown itself openly and admittedly
as the thing it is — a revolution of cruelty, cunning, and

111

despair against the authority and the discipline of the mind.

It is to this disorder and not to some political and partisan dissension, not to some accidental economic breakdown — practical and political matters for the men of politics and practice — it is to this direct, explicit, and intentional attack upon the scholar's world and the scholar's life and the scholar's work that American scholarship has been indifferent. Or if not indifferent, then inactive, merely watchful — fearful, watchful, and inactive. And it is there that history will place its questions.

How could we sit back as spectators of a war against ourselves?

Did we suppose the newly discovered techniques of deception, of falsehood as a military force, of strategic fraud, were incapable of reaching us — incapable of crossing sea water? We had seen their methods drive their conquests through the countries of the world more rapidly than Alexander or Napoleon or Tamerlane or any other conqueror or killer.

Or was it something else we thought? Did we believe others would defend us? Did we think the issue was an issue of strategy, an issue of battles? Did we think the British and the French would win their war and so defend us? But we knew very well, because we had seen, that this war was not a war fought in the open on the military front, but a war fought in the back street and the dark stair — a war fought within the city, within the house, within the mind — a war of treason: a war of corruption: a war of lies. And against treason and corruption and lies, battle fleets and grand armies are impotent.

The questions answer themselves and yet provide no answer. For if we did not believe we were safe by sea water, or if we did not believe others would save us, then our failure to act in our own defense becomes a curious thing. What has prevented us from acting? Lack of courage? It is difficult to indict a generation for lack of courage. Lack of wisdom? There is wisdom enough in other matters.

I think, speaking only of what I have seen myself and heard — I think it is neither lack of courage nor lack of wisdom, but a different reason which has prevented our generation of intellectuals in this country from acting in their own defense. I think it is the organization of the intellectual life of our time. Specifically, I think it is the division and therefore the destruction of intellectual responsibility. The men of intellectual duty, those who should have been responsible for action, have divided themselves into two castes, two cults — the scholars and the writers. Neither accepts responsibility for the common culture or for its defense.

There was a time a century ago, two centuries ago, when men who practiced our professions would have accepted this responsibility without an instant's hesitation. A century ago the professions of the writer and the scholar were united in the single profession of the man of letters and the man of letters was responsible in everything that touched the mind. He was a man of wholeness of purpose, of singleness of intention — a single intellectual champion, admittedly responsible for the defense of the inherited tradition, avowedly partisan of its practice. Where those who practice our several professions divide the learned world and the creative world between them in irresponsible and neutral states, the man of letters inhabited both learning and the world of letters like an empire.

He was a man of learning whose learning was employed,

not for its own sake in a kind of academic narcissism, but
for the sake of decent living in his time. He was a writer
whose writing was used, not to mirror an abstract and un-
related present, but to illuminate that present by placing
it in just relation to its past. He was therefore and necessarily a man who admitted a responsibility for the survival and vitality of the common and accumulated experience of the mind, for this experience was to him the air he
breathed, the perspective of his thinking. Learning to him
was no plump pigeon carcass to be picked at for his private
pleasure and his private fame, but a profession practiced
for the common good. Writing was not an ornament, a
jewel, but a means to ends, a weapon, the most powerful of
weapons, a weapon to be used. Whatever threatened
learning or the ends of learning challenged the man of letters. Whatever struck at truth or closed off question or
defiled an art or violated decency of thinking struck at
him. And he struck back with every weapon masters of
the word could find to strike with. Milton defending freedom of the mind in sentences which outlive every name of
those who struck at freedom, Voltaire displaying naked to
the grin of history the tyrants who were great until he
made them small, Bartolomé de las Casas gentling cruel
priests and brutal captains with the dreadful strokes of
truth — Las Casas, Milton, and Voltaire were men of letters — men who confessed an obligation to defend the disciplines of thought not in their own but in the general interest.

Had men like these been living in our time — had the
intellectuals of our time been whole and loyal — it would,
I think, have been impossible for the revolution of the
gangs to have succeeded where success has been most
dangerous — in the perversion of the judgments of the

114

mind. Murder is not absolved of immorality by committing murder. Murder is absolved of immorality by bringing men to think that murder is not evil. This only the perversion of the mind can bring about. And the perversion of the mind is only possible when those who should be heard in its defense are silent.

They are silent in our time because there are no voices which accept responsibility for speaking. Even the unimaginable indecencies of propaganda — even the corruption of the word itself in Germany and Russia and in Spain and elsewhere — even the open triumph of the lie, produced no answer such as Voltaire in his generation would have given. And for this reason — that the man who could have been Voltaire, who could have been Las Casas, does not live: the man of intellectual *office*, the man of intellectual *calling*, the man who *professes* letters — professes an obligation as a servant of the mind to defend the mind's integrity against every physical power — professes an obligation to defend the labors of the mind and the structures it has created and the means by which it lives, not only privately and safely in his study, not only strictly and securely in the controversies of the learned press, but publicly and at the public risk and danger of his life. He does not exist because the man of letters no longer exists. And the man of letters no longer exists because he has been driven from our world and from our time by the division of his kingdom. The single responsibility, the wholeness of function of the man of letters, has been replaced by the divided function, the mutual antagonism, the isolated irresponsibility of two figures, each free of obligation, each separated from a portion of his duty — the scholar and the writer.

Why this substitution has come about — whether because the methods of scientific inquiry, carried over into the humanities, destroyed the loyalties and habits of the mind or for some other reason, I leave to wiser men to say. The point is that there has been a substitution. The country of the man of letters has been divided between his heirs. The country that was once the past and present — the past made useful to the reasons of the present, the present understood against the knowledge of the past — the country that was once the past and present brought together in the mind, is now divided into past on one side, present on the other.

Past is the scholar's country: present is the writer's. The writer sees the present on the faces of the world and leaves the past to rot in its own rubbish. The scholar digs his ivory cellar in the ruins of the past and lets the present sicken as it will. A few exceptions noted here and there — men like Thomas Mann — the gulf between these countries is complete. And the historical novels fashionable at the moment, the vulgarizations of science, the digests of philosophy only define its depth as a plank across a chasm makes the chasm deeper. That it should be necessary to throw such flimsy flights from one side to the other of the learned world shows how deeply and disastrously the split was made.

That scholarship suffers or that writing suffers by the change is not asserted. Scholarship may be more scientific: writing may be purer. Indeed there are many who believe, and I among them, that the time we live in has produced more first-rate writers than any but the very greatest ages, and there are scholars of a scholarship as hard, as honest, as devoted as any we have known. But excellence of scholarship and writing are not now in question. What matters now is the defense of culture — the defense truly, and in the most literal terms, of civilization as men have known it for the last two thousand years. And there the substitution for the man of letters of the scholar and the writer, however pure the scholarship, however excellent the writing, is a tragic and immeasurable loss. For neither the modern scholar nor the modern writer admits responsibility for the defense. They assert on the contrary, each in his particular way, an irresponsibility as complete as it is singular.

The irresponsibility of the scholar is the irresponsibility of the scientist upon whose laboratory insulation he has patterned all his work. The scholar has made himself as indifferent to values, as careless of significance, as bored with meanings as the chemist. He is a refugee from consequences, an exile from the responsibilities of moral choice. He has taught himself to say with the physicist — and with some others whom history remembers — 'What is truth?' He has taught himself with the biologist to refrain from judgments of better or worse. His words of praise are the laboratory words — objectivity — detachment — dispassion. His pride is to be scientific, neuter, skeptical, detached — superior to final judgment or absolute belief. In his capacity as scholar the modern scholar does not occupy the present. In his capacity as scholar he loves the word — but only the word which entails no judgments, involves no decisions, accomplishes no actions. Where the man of letters of other centuries domesticated the past within the rustling of the present, making it stand among us like the meaning of a statue among trees, the modern scholar in his capacity as scholar leaves the present and returns across the past where all the men are marble. Where the man of letters of other centuries quarried his learning from the past to build the present the modern scholar quarries his learning from the past to dig the quarries.

It is not for nothing that the modern scholar invented the Ph.D. thesis as his principal contribution to literary form. The Ph.D. thesis is the perfect image of his world. It is work done for the sake of doing work — perfectly conscientious, perfectly laborious, perfectly irresponsible. The modern scholar at his best and worst is both these things — perfectly conscientious, laborious and competent: perfectly irresponsible for the saving of his world. He remembers how in the Civil Wars in England the scholars, devoted only to their proper tasks, founded the Royal Society. He remembers how through other wars and other dangers the scholars kept the lamp of learning lighted. He does not consider that the scholars then did other things as well as trim the lamp wicks. He does not consider either that the dangers change and can be greater. He has his work to do. He has his book to finish. He hopes the war will not destroy the manuscripts he works with. He is the pure, the perfect type of irresponsibility — the man who acts as though the fire could not burn him because he has no business with the fire. He knows because he cannot help but know, reading his papers, talking to his friends — he knows this fire has consumed the books, the spirit, everything he lives by, flesh itself — in other countries. He knows this but he will not know. It's not his business. Whose business is it then? He will not answer even that. He has his work to do. He has his book to finish...

The writer's irresponsibility is of a different kind. Where the modern scholar escapes from the adult judgments of the mind by taking the disinterested man of science as his model, the modern writer escapes by imitation of the artist.

He practices his writing as a painter does his painting. He thinks as artist — which is to say he thinks without responsibility to anything but truth of feeling. He observes as artist — which is to say that he observes with honesty and truthfulness and without comment. His devotion, as with every honest painter, is devotion to the thing observed, the actual thing, the thing without its consequences or its antecedents, naked of judgment, stripped of causes and effects. The invisible world, the intellectual world, the world of the relation of ideas, the world of judgments, of values, the world in which truth is good and lies are evil — this world has no existence to the honest artist or to the honest writer who takes the artist for his model. His duty is to strip all this away — to strip away the moral preference, the intellectual association.

He sees the world as a god sees it — without morality, without care, without judgment. People look like this. People act like that. He shows them looking, acting. It is not his business why they look so, why they act so. It is enough that he should 'make them happen.' This is the whole test, the whole criterion, of the work of the writer-artist — to show things as they 'really happen': to write with such skill, such penetration of the physical presence of the world, that the action seen, the action described, will 'really happen' on his page. If he concerns himself with motive at all he concerns himself with the 'real' motive, meaning the discreditable motive which the actor conceals from himself. His most searching purpose is to find, not the truth of human action, but the low-down, the discreditable explanation which excuses him from care. The suggestion that there are things in the world — ideas, conceptions, ways of thinking — which the writer-artist should defend from attack: the suggestion above all that

119

he was under obligation to defend the inherited culture, would strike him as ridiculous.

Artists do not save the world. They practice art. They practice it as Goya practiced it among the cannon in Madrid. And if this war is not Napoleon in Spain but something even worse than that? They practice art. Or they put the art aside and take a rifle and go out and fight. But not *as artists*. The artist does not fight. The artist's obligations are obligations to his art. His responsibility — his one responsibility — is to his art. He has no other. Not even when his art itself, his chance to practice it, his need to live where it is practiced, may be in danger. The writer-artist will write a bloody story about the expense of blood. He will present the face of agony as it has rarely been presented. But not even then will he take the weapon of his words and carry it to the barricades of intellectual warfare, to the storming of belief, the fortifying of conviction where alone this fighting can be won.

There are examples in history of civilizations made impotent by excess of culture. No one, I think, will say of us that we lost our intellectual liberties on this account. But it may well be said, and said with equally ironic emphasis, that the men of thought, the men of learning in this country were deceived and rendered impotent by the best they knew. To the scholar impartiality, objectivity, detachment were ideal qualities he taught himself laboriously and painfully to acquire. To the writer objectivity and detachment were his writer's pride. Both subjected themselves to inconceivable restraints, endless disciplines to reach these ends. And both succeeded. Both writers and scholars freed themselves of the subjective passions, the emotional preconceptions which color conviction and judgment. Both writers and scholars freed themselves of the personal responsibility associated with personal choice. They emerged free, pure and single into the antiseptic air of objectivity. And by that sublimation of the mind they prepared the mind's disaster.

If it is a consolation to the philosophers of earlier civilizations to know that they lost the things they loved because of the purity of their devotion, then perhaps this consolation will be ours as well. I doubt if we will profit by it or receive much praise.

1940.

LIBRARIES IN THE
CONTEMPORARY CRISIS

OUR age, as many men have noticed, is an age characterized by the tyranny of time. Never more than at this moment was that tyranny evident. Those of us who are concerned, for whatever reason, with the preservation of the civilization and the inherited culture of this nation find ourselves in a situation in which time is running out not like the sand in a glass but like the blood in an opened artery. There is still time left to us. But we can foresee and foresee clearly the moment when there will be none.

I do not like epigrammatic condensations of history. I do not like analyses of life which present its situations on the brutal balance of an 'either' and an 'or.' But it seems to me no less than exact to say that the situation which now confronts us in this country is a situation which must be expressed in just these terms.

We face a situation which has an 'either' and which has an 'or,' and we will choose or fail to choose between them. Whichever we do, we will have chosen. For the failure to choose in the world we live in is itself a choice.

The 'either,' as I see it, is the education of the people of this country. The 'or' is fascism. We will either educate the people of this Republic to know, and therefore to value and therefore to preserve their own democratic culture, or we will watch the people of this Republic trade their democratic culture for the non-culture, the obscurantism, the superstition, the brutality, the tyranny which is overrunning eastern and central and southern Europe.

Others, I will admit, see the alternatives in different terms. Six and seven years ago at the bottom of the depression, American intellectuals saw the American progress as a race between *economic* reform and violent revolution. Economics, as you will recall, was then the one, the true religion which explained everything. If you made the economic machine operate, you made everything operate; if you didn't make the economic machine operate, everything collapsed. The 'either' in those days was economic salvation; the 'or' was social ruin. That, however, was before Herr Hitler had demonstrated that men could be led against their economic interests as well as against their spiritual interests if the propaganda were good enough.

Another, and a still popular definition of the American alternatives was, and is, the definition which puts Americanism on one side and a conspiracy of evil on the other. The nature of the conspiracy depends on the angle of observation. To certain good Americans the conspirators are the communists. There was, and there still is, some disagreement as to what a communist is (and some of the disagreement is honest), but there is no disagreement as to the general theory. The theory is that America is all right and the Americans are all right and everything else would be all right if only the communists could be prevented from spreading their insidious propaganda and wrecking the country. It is not, I think you will agree, a very flattering picture of America despite the fact that it is a picture offered by those who are loudest in their protestations of love for the country. It implies that the Americanism of the rest of the Americans is so shaky and insecure, and the appeal to them of communist dogma so seductive, that only by stopping American ears with legal wax and strapping American arms with legal thongs can American democracy be preserved. I for one have never been impressed by the sincerity of those whose eagerness to save American democracy is so great that they would gladly destroy all the American guaranties of freedom to ask, freedom to answer, freedom to think, and freedom to speak, which make American democracy democratic. I more than half suspect that it is not America but some other institution, something very different, something very much smaller, very much less admirable, these people really wish to save.

But the self-appointed guardians of America have not been the only ones to see the American situation as a conspiracy of the forces of evil. The people they hate most, the communists themselves, take exactly the same position. They take it, however, with this difference: That the conspiracy as the communists see it is a conspiracy of evil persons from the other end of the political rainbow. The communist conspirators are conspirators who meet in bankers' dens furnished with black-leather armchairs and boxes of Habana stogies to plot the ruin of the people.

The shallowness and the romanticism of both these pictures of the contemporary crisis are obvious. No one of twelve-year intelligence who really thinks about it believes for one moment that American democracy is endangered by conspiracies — least of all by conspiracies like these. If there is any danger in this direction, it is the danger introduced by those who talk about these alleged conspiracies; not by those who theoretically take part. For the only effect of such romantic talk is to distract the attention of the citizens from the actual situation. Those who shout that America is threatened by the 'reds' prevent a certain number of their fellow citizens from considering soberly and quietly what it is that really threatens America. And those, on the other side, who attribute all our dangers to a Wall Street conspiracy to corrupt the Army and take over the Government, divert the minds of their listeners from the much less romantic but much more disturbing truth.

For the truth is that the threat to free culture and democratic civilization in the United States is the threat not of any person and not of any group of persons but of a condition. Those who, like myself, assert that the threat to a free culture and a democratic civilization in this country is the threat of fascism do not mean by that word what the Communist Party meant by it, or pretended to mean by it, before the Russo-German pact. Those who, like myself, assert that the threat to democratic civilization in this country is the threat of fascism mean that the culture of the Republic is threatened by the existence in the United States of *the kind of situation* which has produced fascism elsewhere, and that that situation in the United States has already given indications, human and other, of developing in the known direction.

The question, the always asking question, the question which history presents to us, and will continue to present to us, no matter how we close our eyes or turn our minds away, is the question how we shall act. Shall we turn our attention to the war in Europe and do what we can to encourage those who are fighting fascism there? Shall we organize patriotic displays at home and punish those who preach fascism directly or indirectly here? Or shall we, as honestly as we can and as directly as we can and as effectively as we can, attempt to change by education the condition from which fascism results?

To my mind, there is no doubt as to the answer we should give. I am aware, I think, of some, at least, of the difficulties. I am aware that the immediate forces which drive the intellectually and culturally dispossessed into fascism are economic forces and that education is not an altogether adequate answer to those who ask for a chance to work usefully and creatively and to fulfill their lives. I am aware also that there are people in the United States who do not wish to admit that there are large numbers of their fellow citizens who have been excluded from the American tradition and the American culture. But I think, notwithstanding these difficulties and objections and many others, that we have no choice but to make use of the one effective weapon we know ourselves to possess. If we respect prejudice because it calls itself patriotism, we are poor patriots. If we wait for the economic restoration of a world at war, we will wait too long. As things are, in the world as it is, we can either attempt to educate the people of this country — all the people of this country — to the value of the democratic tradition they have inherited, and so admit them to its enjoyment, or we can watch some of the people of this country destroy that tradition for all the rest.

It is this issue, as I see it, which is presented to American libraries, for it is upon American libraries that the burden of this education must fall. It cannot fall upon the schools. There is no longer time to await the education of a new generation which will come in due course to a more enlightened maturity. It cannot be left to the newspapers or the magazines, however earnest their protestations of honesty and disinterestedness. There are honest publishers, but there are no disinterested publishers and there never will be.

It cannot, even more obviously, be left to the moving pictures or the radio. The radio's notion of disinterestedness is equal time to both sides, regardless of the sides; the moving picture's notion of disinterestedness is silence. But this burden can be entrusted to the libraries. The libraries and the libraries alone can carry it. The libraries alone are capable of acting directly upon the present adult generation. The libraries alone are staffed by people whose disinterestedness is beyond suspicion. And though there are occasional directors of libraries and occasional boards of library trustees who will stoop to the exclusion of books which offend their social or political or economic preconceptions — books, let us say, like *The Grapes of Wrath* — the directors and trustees of libraries are in general men with the highest sense of their duties to their institutions and their country. The libraries, in brief, are the only institutions in the United States capable of dealing with the contemporary crisis in American life in terms and under conditions which give promise of success. They are the only institutions in American life capable of opening to the citizens of the Republic a knowledge of the wealth and richness of the culture which a century and a half of democratic life has produced.

That fact is a fact which should properly fill the librarians of this country with a sense of pride. But it is a fact also which should fill them with a sense of responsibility. For at the present moment, as librarians themselves have been the first to admit, they are not opening that knowledge and that understanding to the citizens of the Republic. The American Library Association has this year published a small but most important, as well as most readable, study of American librarianship by Wilhelm Munthe, director of the University Library at Oslo, in which the achievements of American libraries in this direction are analyzed. According to such studies and surveys as he found available, Doctor Munthe concludes that in 'an ordinary good library town' the library card holders comprise some twenty-five to thirty per cent of the population; that half of these are school children; that of the remaining adult card holders 'a large portion never use their cards'; that of the remainder of that remainder fifty per cent are high-school students, twenty-one per cent are housewives, two and one-half per cent are business men, five per cent are clerks, five per cent are skilled labor, and five per cent are unskilled labor. In other words, clerks, business men, and laborers using the library in an 'ordinary good library town' amount altogether to less than a fifth of an undetermined portion of fifteen per cent of the population. This figure, says Doctor Munthe, 'is amazingly low.' One admires his restraint.

The truth seems to be that American libraries have executed magnificently the first half of their assignment, as that assignment was defined some fifty years ago by my distinguished predecessor in the Library of Congress. They have solved with great brilliance the problem of getting books for readers. They have developed practices of accession, of cataloguing, of classification, which enable them to secure books intelligently and to make them readily available to inquirers. But they have not executed the second half of their assignment. They have not learned how to get readers for books. The typical American library borrower can still be described by a friendly but informed and intelligent European in Doctor Munthe's words: 'A woman, of twenty-three and one-half years with three years of high school, who borrows in the course of a month four modern novels of no particular worth, one really good novel, and one popular biography or entertaining travel account.' And who are her authors? As Doctor Munthe tells us: 'We can safely say that they are not the ones whose names will some day be cut in marble on the face of library buildings. They are people like Berta Ruck, Zane Grey, and Kathleen Norris. . . . Authors with troublesome or radical ideas are definitely avoided.'

If the learned doctor is right, the libraries of America have a tremendous distance to go before they can feel that they have found the readers their books deserve. But it is not a journey they must make alone. Behind them, far back but still livingly there, are the men who created the American library system. Beside them are the many still alive — writers, teachers, lovers of American liberty — to whom the education of the people for the preservation of their culture is the best and most hopeful undertaking open to our time: the many who believe as I do that we can either educate the people of this Republic to know and therefore to value and therefore to preserve their own democratic culture, or we can watch the people of this Republic trade their democratic culture for the ignorance and the prejudice and the hate of which the just and proper name is fascism.

These are the alternatives our time presents us. They are not alternatives which will remain forever open. We may accept them now or lose them now. 'History,' says Wystan Auden —

> 'History to the defeated
> May say Alas, but cannot help nor pardon.'

History can say Alas to this American civilization of ours as well as to any other. Unless we save it. Unless we act, not only with our words but with our minds, to save it.

October 19, 1939.

FREEDOM TO END FREEDOM

I N AN AGE of political paradox the greatest of
political paradoxes is provided, not by the reaction-
aries who invented the technique, but by the liberals
who detest it. Hitler frees provinces by conquering
them. Chamberlain keeps peace by losing wars. Franco
saves Spain for the Italians. But it is the liberals who declare that the only way to preserve the gentle heifer of
liberalism from the fascists is to shoot her through the head.

They don't put it that way, but it comes to the same
thing. What certain liberals now propose is that the threat
of totalitarianism to free institutions should be met by
limiting freedom of expression in democratic states to
those who believe in freedom of expression and denying it
to those who do not. Specifically, what they propose is
that the privilege of freedom of expression in democratic
states should be denied to the fascists and their congeners,
the communists.

The argument runs something like this: The fascists
and their congeners, the communists, who, incidentally,
are their congeners not by choice but because the fascists
have imitated communist techniques while ignoring communist purposes, do not themselves believe in free speech.
Therefore, they have no right to exercise free speech.
Therefore, the state is entitled to refuse free speech to
them. For if they are granted freedom of speech, they will

use that freedom to capture political power. And if they capture political power, they will deprive others of freedom of speech. And if they deprive others of freedom of speech, liberalism and democracy are dead. From which it follows that a liberal and democratic state, if it wishes to be realistic and hard-headed rather than foolish and visionary, will deprive both fascists and communists of freedom of speech forthwith.

It is a persuasive argument. No one doubts that communists and fascists, when in a position to do so, forbid the expression of views other than their own, and no one imagines that American fascists or American communists would be more tolerant than any other variety. It requires an exceptionally catholic imagination, perhaps, to imagine a communist dictatorship in the United States, but it is easy to imagine what a fascist America would be like. Sinclair Lewis was able to see it in his mind's eye with the most prosaic literalness. A fascist America would not be tolerant. Indeed, Americans being what they are, there is every chance that an American dictatorship would be even more repressive, obscurantist, and bloody than anything Germany, Italy, or Russia has produced. It is one thing to dictate to people who have never governed themselves, or whose experiences in self-government have been brief and footling — people as congenitally subservient and orderly and obedient and patient as the subjects of the old European autocracies. It is quite another thing to attempt to dictate to people whose notion of government is a post-office building, a revenue agent, and the Marine Band over the radio on the Fourth of July.

The nervous liberals are certainly right, therefore, in asserting that American fascists or communists, if they came to power, would suppress the publication of all opinion other than their own. They have done so abroad and they would do so here. Newspapers in Germany, Italy, and Russia are so obviously house organs for the régime that no one in or out of the dictatorships reads them for anything but the light they may or may not shed on the régime's spoken or unspoken intentions. The same thing is true of other forms of communication. The Nazi burning of the books is the characteristic expression of the fascist attitude toward art; and even the Russians, who can hardly be dropped into the same category, have provided unforgettable examples of artistic intolerance. An American dictator who discouraged all American music not based on Swanee River or Alexander's Ragtime Band or Boola-Boola would merely be emulating the Russian dictator who violently attacked the distinguished composer Dmitry Shostakovich in the official newspapers for 'leftist stress of ugliness,' for destroying harmony and melody, and for sympathy with the bourgeois heroine of his opera *Lady Macbeth of Minsk* while granting a flattering interview to Dzerzhinsky, the composer of an insipid patriotic opera based on Cossack folk-tunes and entitled *Quiet Flows the Don.*

It follows that the liberals who would deprive communists and fascists of the right of free speech are thoroughly justified in asserting that the communists and the fascists would have no just cause to complain. People who lay claim to a right only in order to destroy it may fairly be charged with hypocrisy. And hypocrisy, despite the efforts of the British tories to give it international standing and diplomatic repute, is still one of the less attractive human characteristics.

But the argument of the nervous liberals does not end with proof that the fascist and communist concern for civil liberties is pure hypocrisy. It moves on to draw deductions as to the proper policy of the democratic state. And it is precisely there, in that transition from the moral standing of the parties to the proper policy of the state, that the persuasiveness of their argument leaves them. It is precisely in the argument that *because* the advocates of dictatorship have no right to claim freedom of expression, *therefore* freedom of expression should be denied them, that the fundamental liberal paradox appears.

For this transition is what the lawyers call a complete non-sequitur. Its end has nothing to do with its beginning. And the reason its end has nothing to do with its beginning is that its beginning and its end are joined by an assumption that should not be made. That assumption is the assumption that the right of freedom of expression in a liberal democracy is nothing more than a privilege granted by the state to the citizen for the citizen's private profit and satisfaction. Only on that assumption is it possible to argue that because a group of citizens do not deserve, or have ceased to deserve, or have not the right to demand, freedom of expression, *therefore* the state can and should refuse them freedom of expression.

Historically it may be true that the right of free speech, and the rest of the rights guaranteed by such instruments as the American Bill of Rights, were wrung from autocratic monarchs as grants of privilege. But nothing could be farther from the truth than the supposition that these rights are still mere privileges in a modern liberal democracy. In American constitutional theory the right of freedom of expression was thought of as a 'natural right' and the only effect of the First Amendment was to forbid Congress to abridge it. The implication is very clear that the right antedated the Constitution. Today, when 'natural rights' are no longer in favor, it is still true that freedom of expression antedates the Constitution. And for a very good reason. A liberal democracy, such as the American democracy is supposed to be, would be unthinkable without that right and without the other personal liberties commonly grouped with it. So far is it from being true that the right is a privilege granted by the state, that the opposite is the case. *The right is one of the basic conditions precedent to the existence of the state in the form in which the state exists.* It may be — it is at least arguable — that the liberties of the Bill of Rights could exist in some other state than a liberal democracy. But it is certain that a liberal democracy could not exist without the liberties of the Bill of Rights. Popular government without them would be worse than a farce. It would be an impossibility. Unless the people of a self-governing society can assemble freely and speak their minds freely and criticize their government freely, self-government cannot exist.

It is therefore highly misleading to talk about these liberties as though they were privileges granted by the state and had the attributes of privileges. A privilege granted by the state to the citizens for their private profit could of course be withdrawn without injury to any but the citizens deprived. It could be withdrawn in whole or in part. More importantly, it could be withdrawn from one group while still permitted to another. But a right which is one of the foundations of the kind of society on which the state must depend for its own existence cannot be withdrawn in this way. And above all it may not be withdrawn from one section of that society while left in the enjoyment of another section of that society. For one of the characteristics — one of the observed, habitual, realistic characteristics — of such rights as this is that they must exist generally within clearly formulated and universally applicable limits if they are to exist at all. Nothing is more certain than the fact that the restriction of the right of freedom of expression to those holding certain beliefs, and its denial to those holding other beliefs, would sooner or later destroy the right for those holding any belief. The very essence of the right is that it should be effective against majorities and that it should protect the most unpopular opinions. To set up one political exception is to set up all political exceptions. And so even though the exception is phrased in terms of the right itself. It is as dangerous to deny the right of free speech to those who do not believe in free speech as to deny that right to those who do not believe in war or Herbert Hoover or fundamentalist Baptist biology.

The one certain and fixed point in the entire discussion is this: that freedom of expression is guaranteed to the citizens of a liberal democracy not for the pleasure of the citizens but for the health of the state. It makes no considerable difference whether those who enjoy the right of freedom of expression wish to enjoy it or whether they do not. It does not even matter that they would gladly destroy the right if they could. What does matter is that the right should exist and that it should exist in form of right, equally available to all. For unless it exists, and unless it exists in such terms, the kind of state which is built upon its existence can no longer be maintained.

As a practical matter, therefore, the proposal of the nervous liberals comes down to this: that the liberal democracies should protect themselves against dictatorship by an act of mayhem which might very easily become an act of suicide. They should protect themselves against the loss of the priceless right of free inquiry and free expression by themselves infecting that right with death. They should protect themselves against the burning of the books by starting a fire to which books will almost certainly be fed..

This fact should be borne in mind when the supporters of this proposal talk about the extremity of the fascist danger and urge the voters to be 'realistic.' The dangers of fascism do most certainly exist. The fascists, as we are continually told, need win only one election to win all elections, whereas the democrats must win every election to win any other. But though these dangers exist, they are less fatal than the danger proposed by way of remedy. For once the right of free expression has been mutilated from within, the eventual death of liberalism is inevitable, whereas so long as the danger outside in the street remains outside, it may perhaps be avoided. The fact that Hitler was able to use the fifteen-year-old Weimar Constitution to destroy the Weimar Constitution does not mean that an American Coughlin or Long or whatever could use the one-hundred-and-fifty-year old American Constitution in the same way. America is not Germany. The Americans are not the Germans. And being warned by history we are not altogether unarmed.

It is that circumstance which the nervous liberals leave out of account. They do not consider that the classic American doctrine of freedom of speech recognizes a somewhat blurred but nevertheless legible causative relation between speech and action, and permits the state to defend itself from treason, not after treasonable speech has turned into action, but before. They do not consider, further, that the existence of a constitutionally guaranteed right of freedom of expression strengthens rather than weakens the hands of the state in dealing with other practices dangerous to free institutions. The constitutional guarantees of personal liberty and republican government in the United States do not mean that private armies and private uniforms and all the rest of the chicanery employed by the Nazis could not be suppressed in this country. On the contrary they mean they could be, and with the full power of the government.

The truth of the matter is that the necessary weapons for the defense of liberal democracy against the advocates of dictatorship in the United States already exist, without mutilating the one or imitating the other. The present police power exercised under present court decisions should enable a people devoted to democracy to protect their democracy; and the present control of radio, movies and the press should enable the defenders of the existing order to talk at least as loud as those who would replace the existing order with something else. The only doubtful element is not the armament for defense but the will for defense. And it is here that the weakness, not to say the mischievousness, of the proposal to deny freedom of expression to the communists and fascists becomes most obvious.

The will to defend democracy demands a belief in democracy. And belief in democracy demands that democracy should be a way of life with future and unachieved objectives such as men can continue to desire.

If the democracy to be defended is merely the status quo which the great corporations and the reactionary newspapers call democracy when they shout for its defense, then the belief will be cool and the will feeble.

If, however, the democracy to be defended is a future democracy, a true democracy which will admit the failures of this democracy and set them straight — if the democracy to be defended is a free man's way of dealing with a free man's evils in order to create a free man's world, then the will to defend and protect that democracy will be strong enough to sweep over any challenge. But that kind of will and that kind of belief are not achieved by refusing to permit democracy to be attacked. To refuse to permit democracy to face attack is to turn democracy into the status quo and freeze it in a form in which only a small minority can believe.

Democratic belief in democracy, and the popular will to defend it, are achieved only by permitting democracy to face any attack, however slanderous, however murderous, answering the proposals of the attackers with such proposals as a democracy can make. Those who believe in democracy because they believe in the people will have no fear of the outcome. Those who believe in democracy for another reason may very well fear but their fears will be irrelevant.

February, 1939.

THE MAGNA CARTA

THE deposit in the Library of Congress of the Great Charter of 1215 has a peculiar and a deeply moving significance. The Library of Congress is, as its name implies, the library of the people's representatives in the federal legislature. The Magna Carta is one of the great symbols, to all English-speaking peoples, of liberty within the law. The deposit of such a document in such a place is an action full of meaning for our time.

I am aware, of course, that the precise historical significance of Magna Carta is in dispute among the doctors. I am aware that a skeptical generation of scholars has found much to question in the view, so confidently held by Bishop Stubbs and Sir Edward Coke and Sir William Blackstone, that the barons who dictated the Great Charter 'in the meadow called Runnymede between Windsor and Staines' were acting for the people of England to establish the people's rights. Fierce-sniffing philosophers like Professor Edward Jenks, who can smell out the errors of the intellect even in the Muniment Room of Lincoln Cathedral, after innumerable generations of vicars and occasional generations of the vicars' pigeons, have strongly implied that the barons of Runnymede were less concerned for the rights of the people of England than for the privileges they had planned to pocket for themselves.

140

But this dispute, like so many disputes between the doctors, has little reference to realities. The liberties of the people, throughout the popular experience of liberty, have often been established by those who had no interest in the people. It is not important in the long view of history whether the limitations upon absolute power were limitations imposed by a particular class for the intended advantage of that class, or whether they were limitations imposed by popular will. It is only important that the limitations should exist. The far-carrying phrases of the Great Charter may have been meant by their contrivers to safeguard the vested rights of a few landowners and deer-killers in thirteenth-century England. They have enured to the benefit of the people of seven centuries and of continents of which their authors never heard.

No learned dissertation will ever persuade the Americans that the document now deposited in their national library is not a witness to the ancient warrant of their rights. Nor will any amount of scholarly dissension blind them to the meaning of its presence here. The deposit of the Magna Carta in the library of the people's representatives in Congress is a plain and intelligible statement of a plain intelligible fact — the fact, namely, that the institutions of representative government are the protectors, and the only possible protectors, of the charters of the people's rights. For generations past we have taught our children in this Republic that our institutions of representative government were dependent on our constitutional charter for their existence. We have more recently learned, and now believe, that the opposite is also true: that without the institutions of representative government the charters of the people's rights cannot be saved.

There are those in this country, as there are those in

England, who have told us by direction and by indirection that we should abandon representative institutions. There are those who disparage the people's representatives in Congress and who lose no opportunity of publication or of public speech to explain that representative government is not efficient government in a complicated and industrialized society like our own. But though there is much talk there is little listening. For we have been brought to observe, in these last several years, that government by the people's representatives, whatever else it may or may not be, is the one government of which history has record under which the people's liberties have been secure.

Government by the people's representatives, like other governments, can be misled. Government by the people's representatives may, from time to time, mistake, for true defenders of the people's rights, the false defenders of the people's rights — the demagogues, the same in every generation, who appeal to liberty in order to destroy it. Government by the people's representatives may, from time to time, substitute inquisitions and espionage for the equal protection of the laws, and may permit the inquisitors, in their reckless search for enemies of liberty, to break down liberty. But government by the people's representatives is the one government which has never suffered these dishonors long — the one government, in all experience of governments, which has always, in the end, restored of its own will the people's limitations on its powers.

History has many curious and circuitous passages — many winding stairways which return upon themselves — but none, I think, more curious than the turn of time which brings the Great Charter of the English to stand in the same house with the two great charters of American freedom. Thomas Jefferson, who was the true founder of this library as well as the true author of the noblest of our charters, would have relished the encounter. But Thomas Jefferson would perhaps have relished it with a different understanding from our own. For Jefferson was a man who dared to think of history in timeless terms, and of the rights of men as rights which had existed, and which would exist, in every time and every country: — rights which nothing done by tyranny had ever yet destroyed or ever could.

To Thomas Jefferson, the deposit, beside the Declaration of Independence, of this Charter of the liberties of those from whom we won our independence, would not have seemed incongruous but just and fitting — an affirmation of the faith in which this nation was conceived.

November 28, 1939.

THE LIBRARIAN AND THE DEMOCRATIC PROCESS

I T WOULD be a brave man and an optimistic man who would suggest at this hour that the events of the past few weeks and months have been anything but evil. Certainly it would be a very foolish librarian who would suggest that there was any countervailing circumstance to balance the armed successes of obscurantism and brutal force. But there is, I think, one consequence of all this evil which may perhaps be turned to good, and not least by those who keep the libraries of this country. No one can look at Spain, at Austria, at Czechoslovakia, at Poland, at Finland, at Denmark, at Norway, at Holland, at Belgium, and at the situation in Europe of France and Great Britain, without asking himself with a new intensity, a new determination to be answered, how our own democracy can be preserved.

And no one can ask with earnestness and intelligence how our own democracy can be preserved without asking at the very outset how his own work, his own activity, can be shaped to that end. Librarians will ask that question of themselves as others will. And asking it, they may perhaps arrive at certain conclusions as to themselves and their relations to the life of the country which will be valuable not only to the country but to themselves as well.

Specifically they may perhaps arrive at certain conclusions as to the great question which, in speech and in
silence, explicitly and implicitly, has troubled them so
long — the question of their profession.

The wholly admirable attempt to put librarianship upon
a professional basis has, as I understand it, met this
principal difficulty: that it has proved impossible to arrive
at a common agreement as to the social end which librarianship exists to serve. Men are bound together in professions
not because they speak in professional vocabularies or
share professional secrets or graduate from professional
schools. Men are bound together in professions because
they devote themselves in common to the performance of
a function of such social importance — a function so
difficult, so particular, and so essential to the welfare of
society — that it requires of necessity a discipline, a
technique, and even an ethic of its own. The definition of
that function in the case of librarianship has not proved
easy. The social function of the medical profession is
known to every member of that profession. The social
function of the profession of the law was well known to
lawyers in the years before the law became a business.
But the ablest and most distinguished librarians declare
without hesitation that they have not themselves arrived
at a statement of the function of librarianship satisfactory
to themselves, nor have their colleagues supplied the lack.

The literature of the subject, in so far as I have been
able to consult it, would seem to bear them out. Librarians
have apparently agreed at one time or another upon a
description of their social usefulness, but their agreements
have been fragmentary and of such a kind as to increase
rather than resolve the doubts of skeptics. At the time
of the founding of the American Library Association, for

example, librarians seem to have thought of themselves as purveyors of a harmless sort of recreation which would entice the humbler citizens away from 'the street, the saloon, and the low amusement places of the poor.' (I quote from an article by Mr. Sidney Ditzion in the *Library Quarterly*.) Twenty years later this same Association published a pamphlet called *American Library Association Material for a Public Library Campaign* in which the Association gave its blessing to a series of quotations which Mr. Ditzion reprints. Mr. Andrew Carnegie is cited as holding the opinion that the purpose of a library is to 'improve' the masses. Mr. Henry E. Legler supplies the view that the purpose of a library is to 'furnish the ambitious artisan with an opportunity to rise.' Mr. F. A. Hutchins is authority for the proposition that the purpose of a library is to give 'wholesome employment to all classes for those idle hours which wreck more lives than any other cause.' It is at least doubtful to my mind whether librarians would accept these descriptions of their usefulness today. And if they did, it would be even more doubtful that a professional function would have been defined. To provide harmless recreation in competition with the street and the saloon is not a profession: if it were, Hollywood would be a profession from producers and directors down to ticket-takers and ushers in plum-colored regimentals. To give wholesome employment for those idle hours which wreck the young is not a profession. And neither, in any realistic and comprehensible sense, is the 'improvement of the masses.' There are many things essential to the 'improvement of the masses,' if we are to permit ourselves that patronizing phrase, which have no professional implications whatsoever.

Definitions such as these do not of course exhaust the

146

field. There are many more besides. But definitions such as these taken together with the contemporary state of mind would seem to establish the fact that no generally accepted or acceptable definition of the function of librarianship has yet been found. It is to this situation that the disasters of the last few months and their effects upon the American mind would seem to have application. For the destruction of democratic governments in Europe forces us as librarians to reconsider our librarianship, not in a vacuum, and not in relation to ourselves, but in relation to a democratic society ... and, more, in relation to a democratic society which stands in the face of very present dangers.

A newcomer entering the library scene cannot avoid the impression that some at least of those who have undertaken in the past the labor of putting librarianship upon a professional basis began, not with the inward function of librarianship, but with the outward furniture of professionalism — the professional schools and the professional terms and the professional privileges. The kind of reconsideration which danger now forces upon us is a reconsideration which cuts beneath all this to the essentials of our work and of our lives. Today we ask ourselves, not how we can prove that our profession is a profession, but what we can do to preserve and make effective the social institutions in which we believe. More briefly, we ask ourselves what we as librarians in a democracy can *do*. And in the answer to that question, if we can find it, we may also find the solution of the difficulty which has plagued us for many years. 'Out of this nettle danger' said a brave man once. Out of this nettle danger we may pluck not only for our country but for our life's work a meaning it has never had before.

The relation of librarianship to the present and impending democratic crisis is not, I think, impossible to describe. On the contrary, it is implicit in the nature of the crisis. What democracy as a way of government and a way of life now faces is the threat of a competing form of government, a competing way of life, which is more immediately efficient than democracy because it sacrifices to efficiency — to commercial efficiency and to military efficiency — every other consideration, whether of individual freedom or of moral loyalty or of human decency — which could in any way detract from efficient military or commercial operation. What democracy as a way of government and a way of life now faces, in other words, is this — the question whether it can survive in competition with a more efficient way of government and a more efficient way of life which achieves its efficiency precisely by suppressing and destroying and eliminating all those human values which democracy was created to achieve.

Can a form of government and a way of life, in which the basic decisions are made by the people themselves, in the people's interest, and after discussion and reflection, survive in competition with a form of government and a way of life in which the basic decisions are made in secret by a single will? This was the question the President of the United States presented to the Eighth Inter-American Scientific Congress. It is a question the events of the last few days have presented with ever-increasing intensity to all Americans — and not least to those who keep the country's libraries. But to us the question is presented with a particularity and a specific meaning which absorbs all our thought. For the question to us is not the question of public action but the question of public information. If the basic decisions are to continue to be made by the

148

people, and if they are now to be made by the people, not in conditions of peace with margin for error, but in conditions of threat and danger and imminent war with no margin of any kind, how are the people to be informed? How are they to be provided, not only with knowledge of the new facts creating the specific issue to be decided, but also with knowledge of the relevant parts of the historical record which constitute the precedents for action? How are they to be provided with defenses against the special pleading — the propagandas — the new propaganda which now impudently tells them, with all the lessons of Europe spread out for them to see, that they need not act, that no one wishes to attack them, that if they will only delay, if they will only remain weak and silent and defenseless, they will be safe: that if they will only wish to keep out of war they can keep out of war — as Norway wished, as Holland wished, as Finland wished? How are they to be provided with the facts of record, the chapters of their own experience, the materials they must have and have quickly and in the most useful form if they are to decide well and decide wisely the issues upon which all the future hangs?

These are the questions which present themselves to us when we consider our lives and our work not in abstract but in relation to the danger in which democracy now stands. For it is we who are the keepers — the proud keepers — of these records of the experience of our people, these precedents for decision. And it is we, if it is anyone, who will devise means and establish ways to make these precedents available to those who need them. *What* means we will devise, what ways we will establish, it is not for me to attempt to say. I have no doubt the leaders of our profession have long considered this most obvious and most desperately pressing problem and have drafted proposals to submit to you. But of one thing I am sure — that however we answer these urgent, these insistent questions — whatever technical procedures we adopt — the necessity of facing this problem in these terms cannot help but advance our understanding of our work and of ourselves. For no one, I believe, can think of librarianship in the terms of this necessity without a reconsideration of its basic purpose. And no one can think of librarianship in these terms without concluding that the notions of librarianship sometimes held are less than adequate. If librarians accept a responsibility for the survival of democracy in so far as they can assure that survival, if librarians accept a responsibility to make available to the people the precedents for decision and for action in order that the people may govern by them — then librarians cannot satisfy that responsibility merely by delivering books from public libraries as books are called for, nor can they satisfy that responsibility in reference libraries merely by supplying scholars with the materials of scholarship. They must do far more. They must themselves become active and not passive agents of the democratic process. And they must think of their libraries not as patented machines to deliver to the asker the book he wants, their responsibility and obligation ending when the book is delivered to his hands. They must think of their libraries as organizations of intelligent and well-trained men and women qualified to select from the record in their keeping such materials as are relevant to the decisions the people must make and able to provide those materials to the people in a useful form. They must think of their libraries, in other words, not as books and catalogues with the men to serve them, but as expert men to

whom the books and catalogues are tools for the performance of a duty. They must think of their libraries as the
director of a legislative reference service thinks of the books
he uses, not as the director of a circulation service thinks
of books — they must think, that is, as the director of a
legislative reference service who serves, not Congress only
or a legislature, but a people.

That such a service would be as difficult to perform as
it is difficult to define we must of course admit: democracy
is difficult and in no aspect more so than in the provision
of information and the preparation for action. But that
such a service is impossible of accomplishment, we will
no more admit than we will admit that democracy is impossible of defense. To subject the record of experience
to intelligent control so that all parts of that record shall
be somewhere deposited; to bring to the servicing of that
record the greatest learning and the most responsible intelligence the country can provide; to make available the
relevant parts of that record to those who have need of it
at the time they have need of it and in a form responsive
to their need — surely these are not difficulties beyond the
competence of the men and women who have constructed
in this country one of the greatest library systems the
world has seen.

There are dangers in such an undertaking. But there
are dangers also — even greater dangers — in refusing to
attempt it. And the rewards of success are rewards worth
seeking. Not only would the cause of democracy, the
cause we believe to be the cause of civilization, be served.
But it is conceivable that the profession to which we belong might find in the process the definition of its function
for which it has sought so long — a function as noble as
any men have ever served.   May 31, 1940.

AN ANONYMOUS GENERATION

NOTES FROM A NOTEBOOK OF THE TWENTIES

AND the Humanists on one corner and the Classicals on another and the Romanticals on a third and an odd-job lot of odd-job Critics on the fourth and the disgruntled Professors with their Man-of-letters pipes in the windows and all of them orating and pronouncing and declaiming and distressing about poetry, and even the occasional passers-by, the social reformers and the politicos and the doctors and the rich ladies putting a word in, and a whole procession of poets and poetesses milling around from one side to the other in the open street with their thumbs on their pulses and their ears cocked for the Great Revelation and downtown in the National Bank Building a man writing a poem. All this noise is noise. There is a 'problem,' but it is not a poetic problem. And God knows it is not a question between Classicals and Romanticals. Nor between Classicals and Romanticals and Humanisticals. Nor between the whole lot of them and any other organized intellection whatsoever. It is merely the fundamental problem of the location of man in the universe. Poetry, like any other art, can only reach its highest level in a universe of which man is the center. In a human world. And the world centered about man was destroyed by the impulses which produced the world explicable by science. Men lost themselves.

They ceased to know what they were, what they were for. Their position as lords of the animate creation became a very petty nobility, for the animals died and the late-discovered kingdoms of matter and force and time were infinitely greater, more spacious, more powerful, more mysterious than the kingdom of the beasts. The gods of Man held no commissions there. His prayers could not influence the chemistry that ruled his decay nor the fields of force that limited his motions. From thinking of himself as a great king and the object of concern of a great god he came to think of himself as the sometimes expert servant, paid and well paid often, of an unconscious, unreasoning, unbeholden Thing. He accepted the external universe as equal or superior to himself and divided his soul into a million external events. All that remained of the common inner life of men was their simplest emotions.

And since it is the common spiritual experiences of men with which poetry must concern itself, poetry suffered. Eventually it changed. It renounced its world. Each poet became concerned with his own peculiar continent and was greater as that was stranger. Originality, where no other greatness was possible, became the sole greatness. 'Genius,' the poet's exceptional unlikeness to other men, was the final praise. Not the poem but the poem's novelty was the criterion. The only poetry of the common world left to us was a kind of sentimental, ironic, poignant poetry of the primary emotions practiced by persons whose ambit fell within the puddling residue.

Poetry declined. Not as verse. As fine verse has been written by the originals as by the citizens of the great world. But experience true to the poet as a person unlike other persons is not sufficiently true. The Baudelaire experiences of Baudelaire are not true and Baudelaire, great poet as he is, belongs in Literature. There is no body of poetry to give to each part of itself the power of the whole. Each poem is a new beginning. Allusion is a darkening of the scene, for the world to which allusion is made is either the lost world or the unknown one.

There is a 'problem,' but it cuts under the romantic-classic difference. Which is why the romantic-classic debate is so sterile. The issue is between the unified and the dismembered universes. It is not a poetic problem, though it will probably be solved by a poet. The restoration of man to his position of dignity and responsibility at the center of his world — not at the center of one of the arbitrary worlds of science — must first occur. Once there, once seen again, naked on the hull of a blond planet with the sun over him and the stars behind, there will be no poetic problem left. There will be nothing for the medicine men to do.

· · · · ·

In the large square room the bent heads, the heads bowed together, like the heads of people looking for a track through grass, and the voice speaking, stopping, speaking, stopping, running on ahead, waiting, running on ahead. Backward through the mind. The truth lies backward. The truth has been known to Plato — to Georg Wilhelm Friedrich Hegel — to Professor Pollard reading the notes in the margin of his Jowett. The truth is something-that-has-been-known. Plato and Georg Wilhelm Friedrich Hegel and Professor Pollard have known it. They have been included. Trees grow out of them: flowers open as their hands. The low red autumn sun, heavy and round in the metallic air, descends toward the roof across the court. Professor Pollard faces it through the window. He seems to bow.

Becalmed at dusk by the gray cliffs. On the windless sea the shifting of flat light. The gray gull beats across the cliff face invisible but for the rhythm of his wings. The snoring of porpoises passes in the surge to seaward. And suddenly the land breeze, a draught of hot air bitter with pines. The earth breathing, the earth released from the strong sun and alive. The earth alive. The earth is alive at night. . . . It is not true. These are the wooden trees. The touch of metaphor upon the cheek no longer. Pan in a long-tailed derby among the asparagus. Nature, the spayed bitch. We have been into her too deep and too sharp. The magic is out of her and the meaning. The voices that used to speak with authority from brooks and trees, the Voice that with even more authority from a Mountain, the gestures of fleeting goat-form and fleeter thighs signifying at least direction, the half-horse, half-man speaking credibly to man the numb and incredible fact of horse, or half-tree, half-girl performing inwardly the miraculous metabolism of tree into talk, the goddess herself offering between corn-heavy breasts the actual communication with earth — are simply Not. Leaving young men alone with the awkward incommunicativeness of say a hill or an acorn. A long silence broken occasionally by exclamations of surprise.

We have been into her too deep. We have taken the god out of her and only with god in her could she speak to us. God was one like ourselves but having power over nature. Now he is one like ourselves but powerless. Over nature. Over us he has still the power we gave him when we created him to rule both us and her in our behalf; to interpret to our spirits and make reasonable her foreign cruelties and to give material fulfillment to our ghostly wills. Like an aged and impotent king whom habit still obeys he rules us.

His commands, now secretly whispered, though powerless beyond, still trouble us. Our egos, like the egos of conspirators, are exalted by this perpetual listening within. And our wills are defeated because the weight of the defeated will is on them. We hug our spiritual essences and remind ourselves that we are not in nature. We are not only flesh. We have our destinies. No man knows what.

· · · · ·

Alone and without interpreters before the opaque and resolute otherwise of hardened earth, of walls, of doors, of heavens, dig out in words, in paint, in marble, its impenetrable. Force up the living marble into the possibility of knowledge. Here on the blank white page the meaning. The rustling flight of crows at dusk from the fish-rotten beaches. The hickory leaves, shriveled at the edge, brown at the tip, curling into dried shells, and the coarse dusty green leaves of the wild sunflower on the bluff. The south door of the cathedral at Bruges opening to the body of the dead woman; the wall of time. The rearrangement of the furniture in the room making possible.... Bayonne, the wet leaf smell, the wet bark smell, the barges. The negroes undressing with their white wives under the fig tree on the beach. Meaning....

The shaped stone: nevertheless and equally impenetrable.

· · · · ·

The whole law of human thinking is the necessity of believing that of the universe which will make consciousness supportable. Consciousness in an unconscious universe, ignorant of man, obscurely and inanimately logical — consciousness in a universe over which consciousness has no possible control, is the unendurable tragedy. Death, meaning the destruction of consciousness without cure or consolation, is not to be borne. Because he must, therefore, man has believed that the universe was made for him, spirit, by a god mindful of him, or he has believed that the universe was controlled by gods like himself and with whom he could deal, or he has believed that he himself by spells and magic could control the universe. It is not shameful that men have believed these things. Without them we are three-dimensional beings in a world of two, invisible to it and yet subject to it, the third dimension only serving to give us a sense of our fate. There remains to us our emotional conviction that the universe is real. And we attempt to enter it again with our minds, with our bodies, by representations of it in art — we, the intelligent, the forever exiled, who have made our lives outside of life.

. . . . .

The conquest of the cosmos by Science. But it is no lordship. It gives mankind no position of honor. It is no more a conquest than the collection of rain is a conquest of rain. It is a finding out How. You learn what you can do with electricity. A monkey learns what it can do with a nut.

The great modern sickness of boredom has its roots there. We do not wish to be kings. We wish to know How. And we know. And we are bored. To death.

. . . . .

There was one day.... There was a perfectly clear day of off-shore wind and the water was clean and shadowless and ice green and the thumb-smudges of wind were blue over green going seaward and the wind was seaward and the sounds of the railroad yard and the yelping of dogs and her voice singing that thing of Stravinsky's blew out to sea and far out on the sea the shoulders of the little waves were running backward up the slope of the sea with half-hidden vanishing white flanges and there was a white butterfly falling against the green sea and the sun was behind the house and the wind was behind the house and her voice came out through the open window clear as green water, flowing like the loops of light on the ribbed sand in the shallows, fading out like the seaward wind on the sea, leaving the clear green silence. There was that day.

. . . . .

Nevertheless there are endings. . . .

Entering at night upon an almost windless sea that harbor in the Mediterranean, shadowing in across the long slippery reflections of the quay-side lights, the sound of the accordions moving over the water and the long tenor voices from the *Place* under the plane trees — the anchor falling with a throb of chain through the deep water. . . .

December 7, 1929.

DEATH OF AN ERA[1]

THE stair smelled as it had always smelled of hemp and people and politeness — of the decent bourgeois dust. After the linoleum smell of the ship and the harsh, acrid, dampish smell of the boat train the air had a friendly, almost an intimate, taste. Mr. Kreuger breathed it softly as he went down around the caged-in column of the ascenseur. He had a delicate sense of smell for flowers and cities and fabrics and wines and foods. Paris had always this faint odor of hemp under the odor of dust and Cologne water. It was very quiet on the stair on the soft carpet. Mr. Kreuger tasted the silence and the Paris smell. Paris was after all a home — one home — as much his home as any other after fifty years and many journeys — as kindly to return to, say, as London or Berlin or Stockholm — or as Kalmar even with its wooden houses by its milk-blue sea. At the bottom of the stair Mr. Kreuger pushed the glass-paned door.

The March dusk was already darkening the passage, and the window of the concierge's loge was light. Madame Veron, busy at her switchboard among the hanging cages of her birds, looked up to smile. Madame Veron had been sitting there for years, for ten years, lifting up her head to smile. And for ten years Mr. Kreuger, smiling back, had turned the clicking latch to ask for mail, to pat the chil-

[1] From *Ivar Kreuger*, in *Fortune* for May, 1933.

159

dren's heads, to make his courteous inquiries, in his courteous, well-articulated French, for Madame Veron's loud canaries and Monsieur Veron's hardy Touraine cough. But today he did not answer. He heard the sullen traffic on the bridge and the trams go westward on the Cours la Reine. He saw the façade of the Grand Palais. The air was cold with the raw wind and the evening. He stepped across the high oak sill of the doors, stood still a moment, turned to the left, went on.

The street had a strange look, an unfamiliar look, from the wide sidewalk. Mr. Kreuger, in all his years of the Avenue Victor-Emmanuel III, had never walked. There had always been a car at the door, a taxi waiting. But now the distance was not long — not so far as the Rond Point where the Avenue crossed the rolling traffic of the Champs-Élysées. He had seen the gun-store windows often, turning left by the door of Poiret's onetime shop where the rich American women talked along the curb. There was a sign in front like a target with the words 'Tir Gastinne-Renette.' There were rifles in the windows and dueling pistols hung in pairs and English guns. It was a few steps in the gathering dusk — three hundred meters. A clerk received him in the lighted shop. 'Monsieur desires...?' 'An automatic — a revolver — it makes no difference which.' Monsieur was very calm, in no way excited, nothing to make a man suppose... 'Perhaps the 6.35 mm. Browning?' The 6.35 mm. Browning was too small. 'The 7.65 then?' '*Non, plus gros! Plus gros!*' 'The army type? The 9 mm.?' Yes, the army type. Monsieur was familiar with the action of these arms. He was aware of the law which requires the sale of cartridges by the box. He bought four boxes. He gave his name and address: M. Ivar Kreuger, Numéro Cinq, Avenue Victor-Emmanuel III, au

troisième. He dropped the heavy package in his pocket
and went out.

That evening Mr. Kreuger did not eat. He was suffering
from a heavy cold, one of those colds which a March crossing of the Atlantic and a drafty train and a Paris chill can
give a man. He would not admit even to Jeanette, his
housekeeper, that he was ill. He hated illness. But he sat
alone in the furnished salon at the flat desk playing
solitaire. . . .

The morning was Saturday, twelve March, a sunless,
white-skied, pale spring day. In the Salle de l'Horloge over
at the Quai d'Orsay, Aristide Briand, unembarrassed in
death, exposed his ironic face to the long stares of his
countrymen. The Seine, swollen with a Springtime flood,
sucked at the arches of the Pont Royal. There was a cold
wind with the smell of the charcoal stoves blown thin and
gusty past the stale cafés. From the salon au troisième at
Numéro Cinq, Avenue Victor-Emmanuel, you could see the
raw light on the roof of the Grand Palais and the open
ground with its gravel and its plane trees and the new buds
swelling on the trees. By nine o'clock the hum of the taxi
wheels had started on the asphalt and Mr. Kreuger, writing at the salon desk, writing three letters, two in Swedish,
one in English to Krister Littorin his friend, could hear the
wagons on the Cours la Reine. He ended the letter to Littorin — 'Goodby now and thanks. I. K.'

By ten o'clock the noise of the wheels was louder. Over
on the Quai d'Orsay the waiting crowd turned shoulders
to the wind. The Seine boiled back against the pointed
piers. The light blew on the roofs in thin, blank, spinning
tatters. Au troisième at Numéro Cinq a youngish Swede
was rising from his chair. Ivar would not forget the meet-
ing at eleven in the Hôtel du Rhin? He spoke in English,

thickening the words. The tall man at the desk leaned
forward smiling, shook his head. Ivar would not forget.
The door closed. Minutes passed. Miss Bökman, Mr.
Kreuger's secretary, came, sat down, talked briefly, went
again.

At eleven the bell of Ste. Clotilde echoed in the rue Las
Cases and down the Boulevard St. Germain. The doors
of the Salle de L'Horloge were shut against the crowd.
The room at Numéro Cinq was very still. Through the
closed windows the passing cars and the children's voices
under the plane trees sounded far away and faint. Mr.
Kreuger laid his three brief letters on the desk. To one he
pinned a telegram. The telegram had come from Stockholm: Mr. Kreuger was to meet the Bank of Sweden's representatives in Germany on March thirteenth — tomorrow.
The doors of the apartment were all closed. Jeanette had
gone to do her marketing. Mr. Kreuger drew the bedroom
blinds evenly and neatly to the sill. He smoothed the
unmade bedclothes and lay down. The street sounds had
grown fainter through the darkened blinds. Looking up
he saw the fat, gold stucco cherubs in the ceiling corners
of the room. Odd witnesses! He turned his black coat
back and laid aside the leather-covered large gold coin
above his heart. For a long time he had worn it there as
fetish or as guard against some shot, some madman.
Across the river at the Quai d'Orsay the diplomats at
Briand's bier stood looking at the dead, preoccupied face.
Mr. Kreuger snapped a cartridge in the army type, the
9 mm. He placed his feet together neatly side by side.
He shot himself an inch below the heart.

Two hours passed. The telephone rang once, rang twice,
subsided. Jeanette, returned from marketing a little
before twelve, told Monsieur Littorin calling from the

Hôtel du Rhin that Mr. Kreuger had gone out — then later that Mr. Kreuger was asleep. Jeanette had seen him lying on the rumpled bed. Monsieur kept calling, he was urgent. Mr. Kreuger was expected, the gentleman expected Mr. Kreuger and he had not come. Would someone go and waken Mr. Kreuger? Jeanette had called him but he did not wake.

At one Monsieur Littorin drove up himself, Miss Bökman by his side. Together they went in, Jeanette behind them. The room was dark, and Littorin, groping toward the bed, put out his hand. Jeanette could hear him there. She heard his voice cry: '*Il est mort.*' She pulled the blinds back. Silent, his feet together neatly on the spread, his left hand on his abdomen with the thumb cocked upward, his right arm straight against his side, a little blood, a very little blood, below his heart, Mr. Kreuger lay along the unmade bed.

All that afternoon, known only to a dozen unknown men, he lay there. All that afternoon, his bedroom windows scarcely out of hearing — well within hearing if the street were still — of the Champs-Élysées and the humming wheels, the long, neat shape of Ivar Kreuger lay there on the tumbled bed. And all that afternoon, known to the waiting newspapers of the world, the small, dead, humble body of Aristide Briand rode from the Quai d'Orsay across the bridge, across the Place de la Concorde, west by the Champs-Élysées to the Arc, south by the Avenue Kléber to the Trocadéro. After it came four hearses piled with flowers. Behind it walked the representatives of nations. Bayonets every ten meters saluted it. Pacifists demonstrated in its honor. Photographers snapped it from the housetops and the trees. Reporters wrote its passage for the world. Cables waited for its journey to be done.

And when, next morning, the Sunday morning, the thirteenth day of March, the presses of the world ran out their Paris date lines, not Aristide Briand went rolling down their columns to the grief and admiration of mankind, but Ivar Kreuger, *Roi des Allumettes*, creditor of nations, master of finance, lay shockingly, inexplicably dead in two-inch, shrieking headlines on a printed page.

May, 1935.

PORTRAIT OF A LIVING MAN

PEOPLE who like to pick up things by handles have no trouble putting Associate Justice Felix Frankfurter where he belongs. Mr. Justice Frankfurter is the-scholar-on-the-bench. Which is to say that he is the Harvard Law School professor who was appointed to the Supreme Court seat formerly occupied by the scholarly Mr. Justice Cardozo which, in turn, was the seat formerly occupied by that prince of scholars Mr. Justice Holmes, who succeeded to the seat of that scholar's scholar Mr. Justice Gray and so on back.

It is an interesting simplification of history but it misses one fact. It misses Felix Frankfurter. Felix Frankfurter is a scholar and an excellent scholar who has practiced the trade of scholarship for twenty-five years. He is also a justice of the Supreme Court of the United States. But neither the one circumstance nor the other, nor the two put together, can explain the man, or his quality as a judge, or his influence on the country. The key to the influence and the quality of Felix Frankfurter is not his scholarship or his judgeship, but his appetite for life. He is that rarest of God's creatures, a simon-pure, unmitigated intellectual with a limitless relish for living in a human world. He is a disciplined and learned man of books — a man who reads in automobiles and at lunch and at night late and on sidewalks walking — who also loves the fat stews and the wifely breads and the honest cheeses and the common wines of Austrian cooking. He is a scholar of long isolated hours and brief sleep and laborious practice who nevertheless loves human talk and human touch as few men living love them. And it is the love of talk, the love of people, the love of living which explains not only his influence on his friends, and his relationship with his time, but the content and direction of his thought.

It is not paradoxical but quite precise to say that Mr. Justice Frankfurter's theories of the Constitution are theories which derive more directly from his relish for life than from the teachings of his two great masters in the law, Mr. Justice Brandeis and Mr. Justice Holmes. Frankfurter's passion for constitutional flexibility, constitutional accommodation to the needs of live men's lives, constitutional viability as opposed to constitutional restriction, is the reflection not so much of an intellectualized philosophy as of a temperamental and instinctive faith in common humanity and in human life. Few men of any profession, intellectual or other, have believed in the people more passionately than Frankfurter believes in them: no American intellectual of comparable intellectual stature has believed in them as much.

And this belief is not the indolent and insipid humanitarianism which infects certain intellectuals of soft and eager hearts. It is a harsh belief, a discriminating belief, and an impatient passion. The Justice was famous — or infamous — at Harvard for his classroom intolerance of pretentiousness and pose, and stories of his barbed rejoinders from the bench are already circulating in Washington. The empty and pretentious law student, grown to a pretentious and an empty lawyer, continues to resent the inquiry he cannot answer. And the mediocrities of the bar, like the mediocrities of the school, revenge themselves by sticking out their tongues and sneering 'Teacher.'

But Frankfurter, though one of the greatest of American teachers, was never teacher-pedant in this sneering sense. And his taste for people is not the teacher's missionary taste. He loves talk because he loves to talk himself. But his talk is not the professorial harangue. His former students among the law clerks in the present Court give at least as good as they get, and some of them give better. His own clerk, a brilliant black-haired youngster from Kentucky with a wicked gift of mimicry and a sweet-potato tongue, has commonly the last of any argument. The Justice himself tells a story of a Sunday morning breakfast at the big house across the river in Virginia where a dozen law clerks and young lawyers live. There were thirty or forty guests, the food was good, the coffee was hot, and the talk was loud — so loud that Frankfurter's clerk apologized for it.

'Jedge,' he said — the Justice is 'jedge' or 'the little jedge' to the law clerks — 'Jedge, is there too much noise to suit you?'

'Too much noise!' snorted the Justice. 'How could there be too much noise? Have you ever heard me complaining about noise?'

'No,' said the Kentuckian. 'But Jedge! This is other fellers' noise!'

But to do him justice, the little jedge minds other fellers' noise no more than he minds his own. Where the traditional intellectual, the tory of the books, despises men in masses and avoids them when he can, this outward-turning scholar hunts men out. He loves the touch of people. He stands near them when he talks. He catches men he questions by the arm, holding them above the elbow with a gripping hand. He turns the talk of two or three at one end of a self-conscious dinner into a drama of the whole table in which self-consciousness is lost. He moves quickly and precisely from one place to another in a crowded room and suddenly the room is drawn together. He shouts with laughter in a stilted formal silence and the silence comes alive. He writes innumerable letters of one line, two lines, three — 'Have you read this?' — 'Did you see that?' — 'Yesterday I was thinking...' He calls by telephone at all distances and talks endlessly to all hours.

His friends are everywhere and of every kind — tories and radicals, scientists and clerics, artists and politicians, Englishmen, Austrians, Chinese, Californians, Creoles, New Englanders — Professor Whitehead, Sidney Hillman, Doctor Simon Flexner, Bill Green, Charles Burlingham, Lord Eustace Percy, Henry L. Stimson, Al Smith, Beneš, Lothian, Dean Acheson, Harold Laski, Robert Frost, Monsignor Ryan, Bernard Berenson, Albert Einstein, Walter Gropius, Doctor Alfred Cohn — young lawyers, old lawyers, journalists of all ages, tailors, clerks, storekeepers, poets, preachers, doctors — people: people and more people. Some of them are famous; some are not. Some are powerful; some have never thought of power. It makes no difference. Frankfurter will devote as much time to a tailor with a tailor's talk about his fellow men as to a venerable elder statesman with a statesman's secrets.

The influence upon a man's life and a man's convictions of such an appetite for living is not difficult to conceive. A private world would never be large enough, nor a rigid philosophy enough alive, for a man with tastes like Frankfurter's. From the beginning of his career, and despite many flattering opportunities to do otherwise, he has served a public master. And his political and legal philosophy, from the time when he was old enough to affirm a philosophy, has been a philosophy for public life.

Frankfurter first tasted that life at the age of twenty in the year 1902 when he passed Civil Service examinations and took a job with the New York Tenement House Commission as a $1200-a-year clerk to earn money enough to go to Harvard Law School. Before that his life had been divided between Vienna, where he was born in 1882, and New York to which he came, with no word of English, in 1894. Eight years later he had graduated from the College of the City of New York at the top of his class, a small, blue-eyed youngster of abrupt movements, enormous reading, and a gift for public speech. And a year after that, with his twelve hundred dollars in his bank book, he went on to Cambridge, tutored his classmates to make his twelve hundred dollars last, rode up to the top of his class and graduated as an editor of the *Law Review*, the school's ultimate distinction. With such a record he had his pick of the New York law offices and in July, 1906, he took service with Hornblower, Byrne, Miller and Potter.

There followed the one sizable interval of private activity in Frankfurter's life. It lasted two months. At the end of the summer of 1906 the Hornblower, Byrne law clerk was drafted by the new United States Attorney for the Southern District of New York, and from that time forward, with unimportant breaks, Felix Frankfurter worked for other things than private fees. The new United States Attorney for the Southern District was Henry L. Stimson, who had accepted a commission from President Roosevelt to clean up the Malefactors of Great Wealth on Manhattan Island. And Frankfurter's job under Stimson was to make that acceptance good. He did his part. He won the appeals in the Sugar Fraud cases single-handed and gained a reputation for advocacy in the process. Later when Stimson went to Washington as Taft's Secretary of War, Frankfurter went along as Law Officer of the Bureau of Insular Affairs and counsel to the Secretary in his jurisdiction over rivers and harbors — which meant, in part, his jurisdiction over public utilities making use of navigable streams.

In Washington, with a three-year interval on the Harvard Law School faculty, Frankfurter stayed for the next eight years. He held on in the office of the Secretary of War for a year under Wilson, went to Cambridge in 1914, returned in 1917 following the United States declaration of war, was counsel to the President's Mediation Commission investigating labor difficulties, and ended up as Chairman of the War Labor Policies Board, one of whose members was a distinguished young Assistant Secretary of the Navy named Franklin Delano Roosevelt. Thereafter, following a tour of duty in Paris as one of Wilson's legal aids, Frankfurter returned to the Harvard Law School, married lovely Marion Denman, daughter of a Congregational clergyman in Longmeadow, Massachusetts, and made himself the ablest teacher of his generation.

There were numerous attempts to persuade him to go elsewhere. Students in the School just after the War used to guess at the figures offered him to enter private practice. Governor Ely invited him in 1932 to accept an appointment to the Supreme Judicial Court of Massachusetts. And President Roosevelt offered him in 1933 the great post of Solicitor General of the United States. But all these offers, flattering or remunerative or both, Professor Frankfurter declined. From 1919 to 1939, with the single exception of the year 1933–34 when he served as Eastman Professor at the University of Oxford, Frankfurter remained in Cambridge teaching his classes, writing his learned articles, reading the London papers, the New York papers, the St. Louis papers, writing his innumerable letters in his cursive, cryptic hand, telephoning his friends in distant cities, sitting late in the long room in his house off Brattle Street, listening and talking to the three-year generations of the Law School's boys. There was one thing and one thing only he wanted to do. He wanted to inhabit the public world: the world of his time. But he wanted to inhabit it on personal terms, on human terms. And there was no way of doing that which compared, to his way of thinking, with a professorship in the Harvard Law School.

He had his reasons. For one thing, he was a student of administrative law and perhaps its most eminent authority. Inquiries came to him from all sides and from all sources as to matters in his field. For another, he was a man of governmental experience who no longer governed or took partisan positions. Officials of Republican and Democratic administrations brought him their governmental problems. Again he was a close friend of the founders of the *New Republic*, the editors of the New York *World*, the Boston *Herald*. He wrote for all, editorially or under his own name. Finally, he was a former Washington executive to whom present Washington executives turned for the good young lawyers Washington executives continually need; and a teacher trusted by his students whose advice his students would accept. Government officials, judicial and executive, Republican as well as Democratic, turned to him increasingly for their bright young men, and bright young men increasingly went to Washington at his urging.

To the more worldly among Frankfurter's friends, and to the more cynical or the more obtuse among the journalists, Frankfurter's preference for his life at Cambridge had a mysterious, not to say suspicious, look. The cynical and worldly mind has always sought discreditable motives for generosities it could not understand. As Frankfurter's reputation as a public adviser increased following the election of his friend, the former Assistant Secretary of the Navy, to the Presidency, and as Frankfurter's influence spread through the spreading of the men he had influenced, columnists, sniffing for the news behind the news, wrote insinuating articles in which his name appeared. General Hugh S. Johnson, remarking upon Frankfurter's friendship with the President and the number of his former students in Washington, called him 'the most influential single individual in the United States' — implying that his influence was somehow dubious or improper. Other columnists followed suit. Tom Corcoran, a former student of Frankfurter's who had gone to Washington in Hoover's time to work for Eugene Meyer and had stayed on under Roosevelt as counsel in the RFC, was made a symbol of the undefined conspiracy.

Subsequent generations may find these comments curious, not to say diverting. Stripped of innuendo, Frankfurter's crime seems to have been the crime of persuading law-school students, most of whom had gone to Harvard to learn to steer a wealthy client through his tax returns, or to direct a corporate reorganization, to devote themselves instead to the public service. In a country which desperately needs the public service of its best young men, the crime may seem to other generations to have had alleviating circumstances.

Certainly it is a crime to which Frankfurter would plead guilty. And for reasons which go to the heart of his political and constitutional convictions. Frankfurter's convictions are the convictions of a man who believes in human society and its possible richness. They are, therefore, the convictions of a man who believes that public service is the greatest of careers and that it demands and has a right to secure the first abilities. In his admirable lectures on *The Public and Its Government*, delivered at Yale in 1930, Frankfurter openly and explicitly confessed what General Johnson's innuendo less openly implied: 'If government is to be equal to its responsibilities, it must draw more and more on men of skill and wisdom for public administration.' 'In a democracy, politics is a process of popular education — the task of adjusting the conflicting interests of diverse groups in the community, and bending the hostility and suspicion and ignorance engendered by group interests toward a comprehension of mutual understanding. For these ends, *expertise* is indispensable.'

It was in this same lecture that Frankfurter gave the clearest and most precise account of his political position. Frankfurter's political position has been much debated over many years. He has been attacked on the one hand for fathering the New Deal and on the other for not fathering it. His left-wing friends reproach him for taking no position and his right-wing friends reproach him for not taking theirs. But the record is clear enough. The record reads like this: 'Government,' said Frankfurter in New Haven in 1930, 'is itself an art, one of the subtlest of the arts. It is neither business, nor technology, nor applied science. It is the art of making men live together in peace and with reasonable happiness.' Frankfurter's position as regards politics, in other words, is the position of the artisan. He is interested in making the machine of government run. He dislikes dogma as all artisans dislike dogma. He dislikes universal declarations of eternal principle. He has refused to join parties based upon final and unalterable assumptions about the nature of human beings and the meaning of the world. He does not belong among the Party members. He belongs instead in the long and honorable, but not recently honored, tradition of those who think of government not as a partisan's prerogative, but as a wise man's study.

It requires no particular gifts of scholarship to translate these political convictions into constitutional terms and to derive the constitutional position which now gives national and historical importance to Frankfurter's thinking and to Frankfurter's life. A judge who believes that the instruments of governing are instruments, not ends, must believe that a constitution also is an instrument and not an end. A man who believes in the people and who has faith in the processes of human life must believe also that a constitution is a device for living, a device for giving orderly and decent scope to the decent and orderly requirements of a changing world.

In his first year on the bench, no issue before the Court has compelled the Justice to announce in formal and juridic terms so fundamental a conviction. Early in his judicial career he took occasion to refer to the Constitution as 'a historical document designed for a developing nation,' but the remark was *obiter*, as lawyers say, and carried nothing but its English meaning. In several decisions, however, Frankfurter has given intimation of a position of considerable importance to the time. The position is one taken toward the end of his life by Mr. Justice Holmes and noticed with particular approval in Frankfurter's studies of that Justice's opinions. It has to do with a possible difference in the attitude of the Supreme Court toward government 'interference' in the economic field on the one hand and government 'interference' in the field of civil liberties on the other. Holmes indicated that the Court should be more lenient in the first case than in the second and Frankfurter seems prepared to follow. In two cases he has indicated his faith in administrative regulation as opposed to judicial supervision in the control of economic forces. And in one, involving the use of evidence gained by tapping wires, he has refused to tolerate, even indirectly, a government interference with a civil right.

This distinction has considerable significance, both present and potential. There are many who believe that the question which history presents to us is the question whether our existing industrial and economic system can be changed over into an efficient, workable and socially effective system without the substitution of authoritarian forms of government for the democratic forms of government to which we are devoted. The distinction drawn by Justice Holmes and emphasized by Justice Frankfurter has an immediate bearing on this question. For if the Supreme Court can and will permit the legislatures of the states and of the United States the broadest freedom in economic measures while sharply rejecting all attempts to curtail civil liberties, the corner may be turned.

Whether or not Felix Frankfurter will take his place among the greatest of American judges it is not for his contemporaries, and certainly not for his friends, to say. But this much even friends and contemporaries may surmise: that the country now needs, as it has never needed before, intellectual leadership built upon just such a love of living men, and just such a faith in a people's government as Felix Frankfurter has had, and lived by, for fifty-seven years.

February 12, 1940.

GREEN RIVER[1]

THERE were three waves of migration on this continent and the second was always the cattlemen. Ahead of the cattle went the trappers and the Indian traders, leaving a creek's name or a marked tree or a few bones in a huddle of last year's oak leaves. Behind the cattle came the farmers. It was the farmers' plows that edged the drovers westward. And it was the grass by which the drovers went. At the close of the seventeenth century the free range lay around the cowpens on the outskirts of the tidewater settlements of Virginia. A few years later it was in the uplands of the Piedmont. By the middle of the eighteenth century an officer in Braddock's army saw the cowpen men near the headwaters of the Potomac where that stream comes down from Cumberland and makes a gateway to the West. A few years after that there were droves of razorbacks and sheep and cattle in Kentucky. Then the cattle frontier reached Ohio: at the close of the War of 1812 travelers in the Pittsburgh country met droves of thousands of cows and swine from the interior of that region bound for Pennsylvania to fatten for the Philadelphia market. After that there were cattle on the prairies, then across the Mississippi, then at the edges of the Plains. There were always cattle out ahead of the plows. And for a simplest reason.

[1] From *Grasslands*, in *Fortune* for November, 1935.

Beef and pork and mutton were the only crops in that land without roads which could take themselves to market.

Cattle made the first frontier where white men lived. And grass made cattle. Without the grass the settlement of North America would have been a different and a slower thing. But grass, among the histories of the schoolrooms, has no honor. What every schoolboy knows, or thinks he knows, is that the pioneers set out through pathless wildernesses toward an endless forest. That pathless wilderness is a figment of Hiawatha and the academic mind. Long before Captain Smith, long before the historic Indians, the buffalo, transcontinental migrants, had made their trails along the great divides and down into the grazing meadows and the salt licks. In Kentucky when the first settlers saw that land these trails were wide enough to drive three teams abreast. And even without the buffalo the forests broke. The great road of the immigrants, the U.S. No. 1 of American settlement, was the road followed by Lincoln's ancestry: out of Massachusetts to New Jersey, out of New Jersey to Pennsylvania, out of Pennsylvania to the valley of Virginia, out of the valley of Virginia to Kentucky, out of Kentucky to Illinois. It was the road the grass made. The beaver meadows and the water meadows of the Northeast were linked up to the mountain meadows of the passes. The first white men to see the valley of Virginia, by which the great stream of migration from Pennsylvania crossed the mountains, saw endless stretching meadows. And that other gateway, up the Potomac to Cumberland and up Wills Creek to the headwaters of the Ohio and down to Pittsburgh, owed its importance, not, as the schoolboy is taught, to the easy gradients of the streams, but to the oases of grass at Deer Park and Mountain Lake Park and Great and Little Meadows and the Glades of the Youghiogheny. It was the grass in the glades which explained the ancient game trails Washington noted there in 1754. And it was in a grass opening on the Youghiogheny that the Old French War broke out.

By grass meadows and by grazing grounds the roads of the buffalo and of the pioneers went westward with the cattle bellowing down their ruts. From the grass-covered balds of the Blue Ridge in North Carolina out into the highlands of the Tennessee the grasslands straggled. 'Already,' said Burke, speaking of the Americans before the Revolution, 'already they have topped the Appalachian Mountains. From thence they behold before them an immense plain, one vast, rich, level meadow; a square of five hundred miles.' How much more than five hundred miles the Americans had before them the great orator never knew. But even in his day, in 1773, the trappers who for years had unaccountably missed the bluegrass region came upon that empire of a million and a half acres centered on the limestone soils between the Ohio and the Tennessee. And beyond the bluegrass were the prairies. And beyond the prairies, not to be taken by the slowly grazing cattle until the Civil War was won, lay the greatest empire of grass in the Western Hemisphere, 700,000,000 acres of sparse trees or no trees at all, a pasture country greater than the known world in the days of Homer.

Why the Great Plains were a grass country is a question which scientists still answer in various ways. Professor Shaler's theory, which attributed the grass to Indian fires set to start the fresh shoots and attract the game, is the classic explanation of the textbooks. It has few followers today. Soil scientists, a recent breed, remark that, whether in Russia or the United States, the black soils of the grasslands bear only grass. Climatologists observe that grass generally ousts trees in a region of limited rainfall because the grass roots, being shallower, get the water first. But whatever the explanation of the victory of the grass, there can be no question whatever of its completeness. From the blue-stem sod country of the corn belt on west to the blue-stem bunch-grass country of the winter-wheat belt, and on again to the short-grass country of the western Plains the grass, before the white men came, was everywhere.

Most of it, unlike the grasses of the East, was native. The famous Eastern grasses came as immigrants. From 1635 on the colonists were urged to bring 'a good store of claver-grasse seede to make good meadow.' Timothy was cat's-tail grass in old England, herd's-grass in New England after a New Hampshire farmer of that name, and timothy elsewhere because Timothy Hanson carried it from New Hampshire into New York and Virginia. Alfalfa was among the seeds brought into the West Indies by Columbus. Sorghums were the African seeds the slaves ate on their sickening Atlantic voyage. The brome grasses came from Central Europe. Redtop, heir to the classical allusions of the Roman poets, was a native of the Mediterranean. Orchard grass, favored by George Washington, was a cultivated grass in Virginia before his day. Even the famous bluegrass — so-called because of the hazy bluish tinge given to the country in summer by its seed vessels — was an importation. It took on the habit of the country early and became a proverbial signal of rich soil, as hickory was in the Ohio country and blue ash in the coves of the Great Smokies and sunflowers and New England asters and swamp rose mallows in the middle states and juniper trees farther west. Men who avoided

the devil's shoestring regions in the South and the post oak
and blackjack prairies of the Mississippi and the dwarf elms
of the Red River and the purple iris of the Rocky Mountain meadows settled on bluegrass lands with good courage.
But bluegrass for all its fame and for all its eager adapta-
tion to the American countryside, and timothy and orchard
grass and redtop for all their popularity in the old Atlantic
states, were parvenus beside the grama grasses of Colorado
and New Mexico and Arizona and Utah and the galleta
farther west and south and the buffalo grass running down
along the Wyoming and Nebraska boundary into Kansas
and Colorado and New Mexico and the two panhandles of
Oklahoma and Texas.

The short grass of the Great Plains was an ancient grass,
an immemorial sod. It grew before the white men came
like thicker, tougher, coarser lawn. Greening before the
last frost left the ground, yellow by middle summer, curing
on the stalk under the strong sun of August, it had for centuries supported the economy of buffalo and Indian which
was native to that country. Bench after bench, draw after
draw, valley after valley it ran out, tawny yellow, tarnished
golden, from the edges of the prairies to the Rockies and
beyond them. No such grazing country, not even on the
great Eurasian plains westward of Lake Baikal, was ever
opened to the cattle drivers. The pools and trickles and
opening streams of grass which had carried them over the
Alleghenies and down into the bluegrass and out across the
oak openings of Illinois and on by the too rank prairies
here flooded to an endless sea. To General Bradley in 1868
it seemed 'that all the flocks and herds in the world could
find ample pasturage on these unoccupied plains and the
mountain slopes beyond.'

He was not alone in his opinion. In the twenty years

from 1865 to 1885, the Great Plains, which in the north at least had never seen a herd of domesticated cattle, were filled to overflowing. It began even before the buffalo were slaughtered. At the end of the Civil War, with longhorn Spanish cattle bringing $3 and $4 on the range, men in Texas began thinking of the disparity between that price and the $30 or $40 the same cattle brought in the East. The results of that cogitation were the first Texas drives up out of the old ranches in the southwest section of the state to the Missouri Pacific railhead at Sedalia, Missouri. Soon, cattle rustlers, irate farmers, and ordinary thieves on the Missouri-Kansas line around Baxter Springs diverted the herds to east and west — the western wanderers working along the Kansas Quarantine Line, out into the Plains, and north as far as Wyoming. At the same time 'American' (as distinguished from Texan) cows were drifting into the same area from the tall-grass states east of the ninety-eighth meridian: the natural westward movement of migration.

By 1867 the first of the cow towns had been established at Abilene, Kansas, on the Kansas Pacific Railway and four years later the low prices of 1871 were throwing huge herds of unsalable Kansas cattle into Colorado and Nebraska while other Texan herds were following the Goodnight-Loving Trail into New Mexico and on north to Wyoming. Then in 1872 the buffalo abdicated. Under the combined forces of progress as represented by the Union Pacific transcontinental railway, the repeating rifle, and the big-game hunter, those ancient Americans vanished from the earth leaving their hides to the harness rooms of Boston, their skulls to the mercy of the sun, and their feeding grounds to cows.

They were followed in five years by the Plains Indians

whose suppression miraculously coincided with the recovery from the depression of '73 and a rise in the price of beef. Custer was revenged in 1877 by the treacherous murder of Crazy Horse at the Red Cloud Agency, the Sioux were 'pacified,' range steers rose from $7, range delivery, in 1879 to $9.50 in 1880 and $12 in 1881. And the world boom in Western beef was on.

English investors figured that a $5 yearling fattened on free grass would bring $70 and that if the female progeny of 100 cows were kept ten years the herd would number 1428, not counting 1428 bull calves which would be sold on the side for a fat profit. German investors were told the same thing. A certain Baron von Richthofen, writing in 1885, assured his readers that an Irish servant girl of the American West, having accepted fifteen cows in lieu of $150 wages and having branded her stock with her own brand, had sold out the resultant herd to her employer at the end of ten years for $25,000. Money flowed in, mostly Scotch and English money. By 1882 $30,000,000 of Scotch and English capital had gone into Wyoming and the Texas Panhandle. And the money brought cattle. Prairie Land and Cattle (Scotch) ran 150,000 head in Colorado, New Mexico, and Texas on 7900 square miles of land. X.I.T. (Chicago owned) had 160,000 head on 3,000,000 Texas acres and a maturing range in Montana. Even farm cows were brought in from the agricultural states east and west of the Plains. Cattle came from everywhere. And as the cattle came the range grew scarcer. And as the range grew scarcer the rush to occupy it became more eager. And as the rush became more eager the demand for cattle increased. And as the demand increased the price of stock went up. The inevitable spiraling of a great bull market followed. Cattle went up to $30 and $35 on the range in

1882. Tenderfeet piled in from the East, from Europe, from the Antipodes, to buy ranches. A young Harvard graduate named Roosevelt took up a ranch in North Dakota. It was the great age of the range — the decade of the Texas trails and the cowboy ballads.

> 'It was in the year of eighty-three
> That A. J. Stinson hired me.
> He says, "Young fellow, I want you to go
> And follow my herd down to Mexico." '

Grass was the mother and the father of it all. If there was hay at all — which there rarely was — it was wild-grass hay. If there was winter feed it was the winter-brittle short grass which showed its hide-colored sod when the chinook blew. Investments, aside from the investment in stock, were next to nothing. One R. C. Keith started raising cattle at North Platte, Nebraska, in 1867 with five 'American' cows. In six years he put in about 3400 head, mostly Texas stuff, at a cost of under $50,000. And at the end of that time, having sold a thousand head on the hoof for $33,000 and butchered another thousand for $30,000, he had something around $100,000 worth of stock left on hand. The difference between $33,000 plus $30,000 plus $100,000 on the credit side and $50,000 on the debit side was almost all clear profit, for land had cost nothing, ranch buildings knocked together out of old railroad ties cost less than $2000, and men were $50 a month and board. It was no wonder that General James Sanks Brisbin published a book in 1881 entitled: *The Beef Bonanza: or How to Get Rich on the Plains.* You could get very rich indeed on the Plains in 1881 — or, if not on the Plains themselves, why, then on paper. The paper fortunes were huge in 1881.

It was always grass on the frontier and the Great Plains

were the frontier's native country. Grass was their life. It is hard now, with the odor of horse sweat and the odor of gun oil and the odor of saddle leather steaming up from a thousand Western novels, to remember what the grass was. Men took the grass for granted then — and for generations afterward. And yet the grass was everything. It was a natural resource richer than the oil and the coal and the ore which have since been dug beneath it. Even in 1869 the herds it carried were a considerable part of the country's $1,500,000,000 worth of stock. And grass was more than wealth. As no men guessed then, save the few who may have seen the dust dance round the water holes, it was the only living thing that was as strong as drought and wind. Men took the grass for granted. If one range failed there was another farther on — a million square miles of it... The Plains filled up. The herds grew. There was always grass beyond.

November, 1935.

LANDSCAPE OF A PEOPLE[1]

THE Japanese farmer is everywhere; about half the population of Japan is Japanese farmer. But the *life* of the Japanese farmer is not everywhere. It is not to be found in the modernized villages of the Tokyo area, or in the impoverished bankrupt districts north of Sendai where the Japan Current veers off to the east leaving the climate to the icy influences of the Sea of Okhotsk, or in the fat plains south of Nagoya to which inquiring visitors are directed by the Tokyo bureaucracy. To find it in its ancient untouched form you must leave the industrialized areas and the Western-style hotels. You must take the train called the *Swallow*, which drags one second-class sleeper rigged like an old-fashioned trolley and smelling considerably worse, from Tokyo down the Pacific coast of the main island to Shimonoseki at its tip.

You must be questioned by the police at Shimonoseki. You must cross the straits to Moji in a crowded boat. You must answer the police again in Moji. You must elbow into another train with a policeman at your back and run past the great steelworks at Yawata and off south into the southern island of Kyushu which tourists rarely see. You must change trains twice more, each time to the accompaniment of police questioning and police suspicion.

---

[1] From *The Farmer Does Without,* in *Fortune's* single subject issue on Japan for September, 1936.

And finally you must climb the lovely glacier-green Kuma River into the mountains of the prefecture of Kumamoto until you come to a small and undistinguished town of a few hundred houses where you may leave the railroad and strike off fifteen miles up the valley to a village with neither telephone nor telegraph nor automobiles, but with one mail delivery and three visits daily by a spavined bus.

By that time you will be thirty hours and one civilization from Tokyo in a farming village of 285 households and 1663 souls — just under six to the household. It is not an average Japanese village, first, because there is no average Japanese village, and second, because its income and indebtedness figures are respectively considerably above and considerably below the average figures for Japan.

Its entire living scale, in other words, is considerably above the scale of those impoverished northern communities which bring Japanese farm averages down so low. But it is nevertheless very far from a rich village. One family in ten subscribes to a newspaper. There are two radios — one of them in the village school. There is no doctor — two midwives do what must be done. Its most pretentious house would be considered an inadequate summer shelter in Vermont. And its general air is one of careful thrift. Only the loveliness of its green cold river and the excellent circle of its hills would justify its being to the average Western eye. But the inhabitant of a Japanese village has resources which the Westerner does not have. He has the association of his fellows. If he wishes to build a house, his neighbors help him build it. If he wishes a loan of money, he forms a society of his friends to provide the fund. If he must be buried, he is buried by his village, each house sending a woman and a man to cook the tea and beans, prepare the paraphernalia for the coffin and dig the three-foot-square grave in which the dead man, sparing even in death of the village land, will squat considerately.

All these meetings, moreover, even meetings for funerals, are social and human. They are valued as such. If no fitting occasion for a party, such as a funeral or a wedding or a house-raising or the departure of a soldier, offers itself, occasions are invented. And they are warmly celebrated. *Shochu*, the vigorous rice liquor which takes the place of sherry-like *sake* in the proud and spirited south, is a natural encourager of social felicity and *shochu* drunk in the ceremonial manner prescribed by the rules of politeness is an encourager of even more. After having saluted each of thirty guests in the thimblefuls of village etiquette, honored grandfathers will throw back their heads and sing the songs of congratulation, severe fathers will dance ancient village dances of the catching of fish or the bereavement of parents, and a blunt sexuality will overtake the entire gathering which is too frank to be obscene and too open to be indecent, but which is nevertheless a sharp gulp in the throat to the Western watcher.

What sticks in the mind, however, is not the ribald gesticulating of these gatherings, but their humanness, the sense of common life, the recognition of an interdependence and mutual responsibility which has long been lost from the West. The poor man in the West will not be allowed to starve. But the poor man in the Japanese village has much more than this negative and grudging security. He is part of the life of many men and his destiny is theirs. The whole village is together. In the celebrations of the popular religions, costumes and the beating of drums and the chanting of songs and the swinging of torches fuse many men together into the half-hypnotized, half-drunken one-man of a crowd. In the pilgrimages to shrines and temples and the expeditions to 'view' famous cherry woods or growths of iris or chrysanthemums or autumn grasses, briefer but no less satisfying crowdings and jostlings of humanity are brought about.

The density of the people gives a continuing sense of common life. The absence of walls is real. In the village street at night the voices of children, chanting as they read, come from behind the glowing rice paper as though there were no division between. Men and women, indoors and out, speak back and forth without raising their voices. A passer-by will stand a moment to gossip with a bather chest-deep in his tub a few strides from the road, the soft light of a wick flickering over his naked shoulders.

The picture is idyllic. To the Westerner with his nostalgic, deep-buried memories of a vanished village life — a closely integrated, warm, and human life in the far-off, unrecoverable racial past — it is too idyllic. There are no margins in the farming country in Japan — no margins either of land or rice or money. There is no room for margins. Half the farming households cultivate less than an acre and a quarter of rice. Three-quarters of them cultivate less than two acres and a half. Only one man in a thousand has the 157 acres which the average American farmer uses. Nowhere else in the world is there such a concentration of humanity upon arable land as in the main island of Honshu and the southern islands of Kyushu and Shikoku where all but three or four of Japan's seventy millions live. One acre out of seven in that country of up-edged mountains breaking away into pockets of useful earth will grow food. Twenty years ago each seventh acre was producing food for four human mouths. Today with a population a quarter again as great it must feed five or six.

The swollen population is already piled up 2995 deep on the square mile of food-producing land.

The consequence is the landscape of Japan. It is a landscape more human than almost any other in the world. It tells more of the lives of men. It describes a country scoured by humankind, a country where the loam has been sifted through human fingers of one blood, generation after generation, until even the rain on the dust smells of humanity, a country where the fields are too narrow for the men who feed upon them, and where, for centuries, those who ate were weeded out till they matched with that which could be eaten. *Mabiki*, which was the word for infanticide in those days, was also the farmer's word for thinning out a crop. The landscape of Japan is the landscape of a country where the struggle of men with the earth has been turned wrong side to — where the struggle has been, not to subdue the earth to men, but to subdue the needs of men to the capacity of the green fields.

September, 1936.

OF MANY MEN ON LITTLE
LAND[1]

WESTERNERS recognize the landscape of Japan in the delicate prints by a few simple indications — by Mount Fuji with its symmetrical icing or by a cherry tree or by plucked-looking, wind-warped pines silhouetted on the ragged ridgepole of a mountain, or by the straw roofs made to slant as hills do.

There are other signs for those who look to see them.

There are the roads always narrow and mostly at the wood's edge or the river's.

There is the straw piled on brushwood bridges off the loam and the trees only growing at the god's house, never in the fields.

There are the whole plains empty of roofs, squared into flats of water, no inch for walking but the dike backs, not so much as a green weed at the foot of the telegraph poles or a corner patch gone wild.

There are the fields empty of crows after harvest: thin picking for black wings after cloth ones.

There are the men under moonlight in the mountain vil-

[1] From *Of Many Men on Little Land* in *Fortune's* single subject issue on Japan for September, 1936.

190

lages breaking the winter snowdrifts on the paddles to save days of spring.

There are the forest floors swept clean and the sweepings bundled in careful, valuable piles.

There are the houses without dogs, the farms without grass-eating cattle.

There are the millet fields at the sea's edge following the sweet water to the brackish beginning of the salt, the salt sand not the thickness of a stake beyond.

There are the rivers diked and ditched and straightened to recover a napkin's breadth of land and the hill valleys terraced till the steepest slope turns flatwise to the sun.

There are the mountains eroded to the limestone where the axes and the mattocks have grubbed roots.

All these are in the landscape. And all these — the cheese rind eaten to the brittle crust above and the careful hoarding of the crumbs below — are like Japan.

Japan is the country where the stones show human fingerprints: where the pressure of men on the earth has worn through to the iron rock.

There is nothing in Japan but the volcanoes and the volcanic wastes that men have not handled. There is no getting away from men anywhere: from the sight of men in the open houses or from the shape of their work in the made fields or from the smell of their dung in the paddy water.

In other countries a farm is meadows and a wood lot and a corner that the plow leaves: room to turn about and time to turn about in. In Japan a farm is as rigid and tight a thing as a city lot — a patch here and a triangle there and a square or so somewhere else: every road corner of land diked and leveled off even though the growing surface is less than a man's shirt; every field soaked with manure

191

and worked and reworked as carefully and as continuously as a European farmer works a seedbed . . .

. . . nothing thrown away, nothing let go wild, nothing wasted.

September, 1936.

POSTCARDS AND
HACIENDAS[1]

☆

I N CHILE, as elsewhere on this earth, there are two kinds of observations to be made. There are the observations for the picture postcards, with the volcanoes over the lakes and the cordillera over the poplars. And there are the observations for the reports of the vice-presidents of banks.

For the postcards there are the observations: that the direction of the prevalent wind on the Atacama Desert is shown, not by the trees, for there are none, but by the insulators on the power line blown all one way together ... that the Chilean sense of humor is as dry and sardonic as the humor of the state of Maine ... that Santiago in the year 1938 smells of wet cement and fresh paint and sawed lumber, and that the new modern-style office buildings look even newer than they are in that city of streets ending in mountains ... that the Chilean sun, jarring the air above the naked nitrate pampas, is like an act of violence on the earth, and that the Chilean shadow is cool, clear, and light as a morning in autumn ... that Chile is one of the ancient countries of the earth with its oxen out of the Old Testament and its fruits fragrant as the fruits of Homer and its mountains like the mountains at the begin-

[1] From *South America, III: Chile*, in *Fortune* for May, 1938.

ning of time... that the shops at Concepción are filled
with Chilean shirts and Chilean shoes and Chilean note
paper and that even the American toothpaste with the
American label is made in Chile... that the slums of
Santiago and Rancagua are as bad as the slums of Brook-
lyn and Chicago... that the funerals of children (the little
body folded in the shapeless box) are everywhere in the
afternoons. There is the observation, also, that the smell
of poverty in Chile is the thin smell of thorn twigs and
eucalyptus burning in the petrol cans for stoves.

But the observations which will hold the attention of
the receivers of postcards will not hold the attention of
the vice-presidents of banks. To the vice-presidents of
banks, observations, to signify, must illustrate the condition of the national economy. Of such observations in the
Republic of Chile there is chiefly one. There is chiefly
the observation that the lady tourists from Argentina go
bathing in the harbors where the nitrate used to load.

This observation, which goes somewhat deeper into the
present economy of Chile than the vice-presidents of the
banks find it politic to go, may be verified any summer
morning on the second-story, rickety balcony of the Hotel
Maury in Antofagasta. What you will have before you,
sitting there with your feet on the shaky railing staring at
the sea, is the immense intensity of sunlight where, a generation ago, twenty or thirty ships lay in together loading
nitrates from the lighters through the surf, fouling the
harbor water with their garbage and their oil. What you
have before you now is a single German freighter yanking
at her cables in the swell, and close in, wading through the
shallow atmospheres of water on the rocks, bathing with
their arms and bodies floating in the clear transparent
pools, the Argentine Italians down from Salta....

For fifty years, from the eighteen-eighties on down to the nineteen-thirties, Chile was a sort of elegant remittance man among the nations of the earth. Year in and year out she received her average royalty of $25,000,000 from nitrate fields largely operated by foreigners. Nitrates paid up to 68 per cent of her costs of government, relieving her ruling-class landowners of the unpleasant necessity of imposing taxes on themselves. Nitrates produced a steady flow of foreign exchange for the purchase of manufactured goods from abroad, making it unnecessary for the republic to create its own manufacturing industries. Nitrates thus permitted the Chilean landowners to retain on their vast estates a medieval economy with practical serfdom for their laborers and European educations for their numerous families of blond and lovely daughters and aristocratic sons.

The one statement about the Chilean nation which can be made without fear of contradiction from anyone is the statement that it is two nations. But *which* two nations is not so certain. In the upper-class view it is two nations racially. The great aristocratic families think of themselves as Basques who came to Chile in the eighteenth century to run the country or to trade, married into the families of the conquistadors, took over their lands, accepted accretions of English, Irish, Scotch, and French blood, and are today more English, Irish, Scotch, and French than Spanish; and they think of the masses of the people as descendants of Andalusian soldiers and women of the proud and warlike Araucanian Indian race. In the lower-class view, on the other hand, the two nations are the two nations of Disraeli, divided by a frontier not of blood but of wealth: there is no more Indian blood in one part of the population than in the other. For the lower class, Chile is divided into the rich and the poor.

The foreigner in Chile may take his choice between the opposing theories. He will probably conclude that there is a certain element of truth in each. Certainly the great families of Chile are more North European than Spanish or Indian in appearance. Though they speak Spanish with the accent of Seville their names are as often as not English or Scotch or Irish — Lyon, Mackenna, Edwards — and where they are Iberian names they are frequently Basque names from the north — Larraín, Yrarrázaval, Errázuriz, Ochagavía, Echenique. Their faces are Celtic or Anglo-Saxon or Basque, with clear features and frank eyes. The complexions of the women are often as blond as those of the blondest Englishwomen. And the general impression seems to have more to do with the old families of New York, Philadelphia, and Boston than with any conceivable group of Latins.

It is therefore undoubtedly true that there are racial differences between the members of the great landholding families and the masses of the people. But, if so, it is the masses of the people who are the true Chileans — for it is the masses of the people who are Latin. Aside from the descendants of the German farmers who began settling in and around Valdivia in the eighteen-fifties and who thought of themselves as Chileans until Hitler enunciated his theory of the immutability of the German germ plasm, and aside from the Italians and Syrians and Turks in the grocery stores, and the gringos in the banks, the lower and middle classes in Chile are as Spanish in complexion and looks as their masters are Celtic and Basque and Anglo-Saxon. . . .

Nothing on the American continents is more remote in time than the look and feel of an old Chilean hacienda in

the great irrigated central valley of Chile, with the mari-
time mountains to the west and the snow-edged cordillera
to the east, and the family lands running on and on, poplar break after poplar break, as far as a man can see.
Here nothing has changed in generations save that the old
original grant has been divided once or twice by inheritance, and a Deere tractor works beside the oxen.

The alfalfa comes in on two-wheeled ox-drawn carts
with an *inquilino* [1] balancing on the lurching load, and
the ten kilo cheeses stand on the sagging shelves in the
stone-cool rooms, and the brood mares with the foals
against their flanks come home between the poplars in the
lovely luminous shining of the twilight dust, and the huge-
necked Holstein bulls loaf with the cynical detachment of
the no-longer-wishing male, and the cordillera runs in a
savage impenetrable beauty beyond the soft familiar
humanness of the willow trees, and the pasture smells at
evening of mint and irrigating water and dry straw. The
inquilinos are what they were generations ago. Their
houses are a little better. Their pay is a little higher. But
they are still the manservants and maidservants of the
Old Testament, humble, hopeless, and obedient. And the
houses of the *hacendados* are still the low, spreading,
patriarchal houses with their sixty bedrooms, and their
family chapels, and their flowery courts, and their dinners
of ten and fifteen and twenty and thirty together, and their
iron-barred windows, and their enormous dogs. In summer on the great haciendas, with the *hacendado's* family
out from Santiago for the holidays, and the mornings all
sun and clear air and lightness of heart, and the hoofs of
the saddle horses in the courtyard in the afternoon, and
the long teas, and the heavy tables, and the evenings under

[1] The semi-feudal farm laborer attached to the hacienda.

the cordillera and the stars, and the dinners at half-past nine, and the drowsy talk, and the bolted shutters, and the hot baths at midnight, and the heavy sleep — in summer on the haciendas time turns backward toward a past as far away as childhood.

But there is another side to this pastoral life. There is the literature and then too there is the fact. There is the harvest of the nectarines, the murmur of voices under the cool trees, the fragrance of fruit, the sun steep, strong, and burning like another presence in the air. And there is the eight-peso wage of the nectarine pickers. There is the *trilla* — the threshing of wheat under the hoofs of horses with the herd of twenty or thirty driven round and round within a ring of straw, the easily loping *huasos* behind them shouting '*Ah yegua! ah yegua!*', the horses running shoulder to shoulder with the colts ahead and the sweet dry smell of the crushed straw in the sun, and when the sound dies down the same cry from beyond the poplars in another field. There is the *trilla* — and there are the heavy faces of the *inquilinos* with their pitchforks in the center of the ring. There is the green wine also, and the girl in the black, coarse dress, her beautifully moving, rich, full woman's body eloquent as she lifts the pitchers. And there are the milking women in the stables with the hopeless eyes.

May, 1938.

THE ART OF THE GOOD
NEIGHBOR

THERE are phrases which can be pronounced only in quotation marks. 'Cultural relations' is one of them. Cultural relations are not something you have: they are something you read about having. Generally they are something you read about having with considerable reluctance. The average citizen may be willing to put up with the man who writes about United States cultural relations with Latin America meaning thereby United Fruit. He is not likely to put up with the man who writes about United States cultural relations with Latin America meaning thereby precisely what he says. History is against it. History is the context in which language is understood, and history in this case is unobliging: it calls back the bonds of Minas Geraes, the capitalization of Cosach, and the marines at Vera Cruz. It makes the phrase sound awkward.

And nevertheless the awkward phrase is honest. It stands for serious things. It stands for the realization of informed persons that the present struggle of the propagandas in Latin America is a struggle for something more than markets. In that division of the Department of State where Ben Cherrington and Charles Thomson labor ably for the light, it stands for the realization of a particularly

perceptive Under Secretary and a particularly imaginative Assistant Secretary that the German press and radio
attacks on the United States in Latin America are not
attacks for economic ends alone.

There was a time when the professional understanders
understood that the great division which splits the world
was a division between those who Had on the one side and
those who Had Not on the other. Those who Had Not
wanted the wealth and the markets and the raw materials
and the colonies of those who Had. It was as simple as
that. Nothing was at stake in the great unexploited market areas or the great undeveloped raw-material areas but
goods and things. Those who interpreted Latin American
affairs by this simple light interpreted them in these simple
terms. If the Germans disparaged American culture on
the short wave or by word of mouth or by special articles
in the Valparaiso press, they were doing it for economic
reasons only. If inspired publications discovered that the
civilization of the North Americans was debased, was materialistic, was Bigbusiness, was vulgar, was artless, was
crass, had produced no poets, had bred no painters, had
trained no scholars, all this was no more than a diversion,
a flank movement in the great war for trade. The Germans, lacking the credits to fight the Americans on the
loading quays and in the grain elevators and at the banks,
were undermining them at the dinner tables of the haciendas and the estancias and the high shiny apartment
houses over the River Plate.

That simplification of history however, like all such
simplifications of the ancient record, was less than wholly
satisfying to imaginative minds. Events in distant parts
of the earth suggested that the great division on the basis
of the verb to have was not necessarily the true division

of our time. Events in distant parts suggested that the purposes of those who bombed the Spanish towns and shot the Czechoslovak students were not economic purposes alone but purposes of a more ambitious character. What was under attack was not merely the present title to the riches of the world. What was under attack was the entire moral and intellectual and artistic order which, by accident or otherwise, was associated with that title.

Which meant, first, that the flank attack on the culture of the North Atlantic democracies in Latin America was perhaps not a flank attack at all but the principal engagement. And which meant, second, that those who had regarded the struggle with indifference so long as it seemed to be a struggle between the fat and the lean for the cut of the meat, could no longer regard it with indifference. Men in the United States who cared not at all whether Germany rather than Great Britain exploited the people of India, cared a great deal whether the civilization based upon free inquiry and free imagination which had developed in Western Europe and across the Atlantic over several centuries survived or perished. A change which put the Germans in Tanganyika was one thing. A change which burned the books of Thomas Mann in America also, and disciplined the composition of Szostakowicz here as well as in the Moscow theatres, and murdered Garcia Lorca not only in Granada but in New York, and organized the natural sciences on the party line not only in Siberia but in the Western Hemisphere as well, would be another.

It is to this altered understanding of the nature of the struggle that the awkward phrase relates. The movement to promote cultural relations between this country and Latin America is not at all the hypocritical and missionary movement which history would suggest. It is the precise opposite of a missionary movement. It does not aim to bestow upon a backward people below the Rio Grande the rich gifts of our superior culture. It aims instead to defend our culture against attack in the area where our culture is most in danger. To that end it labors to persuade the artists and intellectuals of the Spanish- and Portuguese-speaking nations of the American continents that a North American culture exists, that it is a culture worthy of admiration, and that the substitution of a different cultural influence in the Americas might be the substitution of a worse.

In Chile and Brazil and Argentina and Colombia as in few other parts of the world nations are judged by their cultural achievements. And in Chile and Brazil and Argentina and Colombia judgments of cultural achievement are determined to an unusual degree by the opinions of the competent intellectuals. When we attempt to persuade the Latin American nations that the achievements of our culture are admirable, we are not attempting to persuade a million magazine readers or ten million radio listeners or the sampled public of a 'scientific' poll. We are not, in other words, attempting to persuade the people as the people are occasionally persuaded at home by magazine publishers or advertising agencies. We are attempting to persuade a small and sophisticated and discriminating jury of critics and artists and professional scholars: a specific group of known and distinguishable people — the eminent critic of modern verse in Buenos Aires pacing the long room over the earthen river — the authority on modern music in the garden of enormous trees under the mountains of Santiago — the lady in the chair at Miraflores, the words dissolving in the dissolving light, the fame hanging there.

To attempt to persuade a jury such as this, not by facts but by works, not by propaganda but by the submission of the documents — the books, the poetry, the music, and the painting — is neither hypocritical nor self-righteous. It is, on the contrary, an exceedingly frank and forthright undertaking. It is also an undertaking as difficult as it may be dangerous.

The difficulty is obvious enough. The jury to which, with a sudden gesture of respect, we now prepare to submit the products of our culture is a jury already prejudiced against them. Long before the Nazis began their unflattering descriptions of our writers and painters and architects and actors and scientists and men of learning, the intellectuals of Latin America had concluded that our writers and our men of learning were men of small account. There was every reason why they should. We had ourselves gone to considerable lengths to persuade them that our culture was the culture of the Grace Line, the National City Bank, the Hearst comics, the Hollywood heart-throb, and an occasional best-seller. And there were no ready means by which they could correct that impression for themselves.

In terms of cultural, as distinguished from physical, geography, Latin America is a foreshore of Western Europe and particularly of the city of Paris. A Chilean critic knows North American writers as they are known in Paris — or rather as they are known in those Parisian porches which open upon the Spanish-speaking world. He knows American music not at all. And if he sees American painting, he sees it only in the colored reproductions of the magazines. All he can say of American arts and letters is that his friends in the American colonies in Santiago and Buenos Aires do not speak of them, that the notes in his Paris and Madrid reviews ignore them, and that he has never seen them for himself. A few men of exceptional intellectual curiosity, like Mallea of *La Nación*, may read widely among North American novelists and poets, but they are the exceptions, as their counterparts would be exceptions here.

It is this quite natural prejudice of the jury to which we have appealed which creates the difficulty of the undertaking. Excellence exists, and if we will offer it with tact and taste we will persuade even a jury prejudiced as this is. But mediocrity and vulgarity also exist and in superior quantities with superior influence and more numerous friends. If those who have made themselves responsible for the furtherance of this enterprise permit — and it will be difficult not to permit — our 'cultural relations with Latin America' to become the property of trading corporations with advertising programs to put over, or of self-appointed groups of culturists with careers to make, or creeds to propagate, or fads to follow; or if those who have initiated this undertaking lose interest in it and fail to push it through, letting the Latin American audience they have prepared wait with a growing boredom for cultural revelations which fail to come, the prejudice will soon become a final, ineradicable, and articulate conviction.

The difficulty then is plain. And the danger follows. Whether we intended to do so or not, we have now undertaken, and undertaken through official agencies, to present to the people of Latin America convincing proofs of the creativeness and vitality of our culture. To fail would be disastrous. And yet no one, I think, considering the facts, can fail to conclude that these commitments have been given without adequate assurances beforehand of the co-operation of those whose co-operation is essential — the handful of true artists and true scholars who alone can enable us to perform these promises; without proper guaranties against the interference of the mediocrities and vulgarians — the fashionable favorites, the smart names, the false bosoms — whose interference would make our promises ridiculous; and without a realistic count of the cost of failure.

Briefly and specifically, the initiators and promoters of this program have put not only themselves, and not only the artists of this country, but the country itself in a position of considerable danger from which the only possible retreat is forward. If the cultural relations of peoples were what our uncles and grandfathers thought them — diversions, decorations, and irrelevancies — failure in this present undertaking would be mildly shameful and no more. But in a divided world in which the real issue of division is the cultural issue, cultural relations are not irrelevancies. They are everything. And in such a world a cultural defeat is a defeat on the one front on which defeat cannot be accepted.

Simplifications are suspect in our time, but there is one simplification which may surely be advanced. Unless the civilization which rests upon free institutions and personal liberty can justify itself *by its works* in those areas in which it is pressed by a competing order, it will not justify itself by other means. We shall do well to recognize that fact, to realize that we have committed ourselves to a hazardous and costly venture, and to attempt now, before it is too late, to make good on our commitments.

February 10, 1940.

ARGENTINA OF THE PLATE:
ARGENTINA OF THE PAMPAS[1]

☆

THERE are two views of Argentina. One is down the Diagonal Norte in Buenos Aires with the foreground full of leather-upholstered Buick touring cars tricked out as taxis, the middle distance full of the glass windows of expensive new office buildings, and the far distance vanishing down endless streets into a faint and unseen haze of prairie. The other view is in reverse. It may be enjoyed from various spots in the country: among others from the afterdeck of the side-wheeler *General Artigas* as she walks her three-day way up the Parana River from Buenos Aires to Barranqueras. Hours after the *General Artigas* has left the muddy, fresh-water swells of the estuary of the Plate, hours after the last of the daylight has lifted from the flint-colored river and Italian señoritas from Rosario have shut the piano in the ten-foot saloon and kissed their enormous mothers and gone to bed, hours after the Paraguayan law student with his right arm buried in the Chaco has stopped his narrow nervous circling of the upper deck and the plump Argentine chaplain in the god-hunter's hat has retired from the table of the melancholy lady from Resistencia — hours after the whole ship has settled down to

[1] From *South America, IV: Argentina*, in *Fortune* for July, 1938.

listen to the slapping of the paddles on the sullen, silent water, you can see this second Argentina. One side and the other and ahead the plain goes on and on, flat at the level of the eye, enormous in its emptiness and silence, and far back, swinging as the boat swings, small, portentous, and alone, the city burns its bonfire on the margin of the night.

If you take the first view of Argentina — and most tourists, a considerable number of interested financiers, and not a few diplomats take it — you will end up with one conclusion. Buenos Aires is a great city. It is a great city on any basis. It is a great city as the ancients measured great cities: a strong town famous for the horsemanship of its men and the beauty of its women. It is a great city in the sense in which Paris and New York are great cities. It is a cosmopolitan, twentieth-century metropolis with all the fixings — crowds, avenues, parks, subways, visiting pianists, confusion of tongues, screaming of brakes, shining of movie theatres, braying of radios, dancing of ankles, seduction of mascara'd eyelashes in the mirrors of cream-upholstered Cadillacs, impudence of plaster-of-paris bosoms in the show windows of lingerie shops, cadenzas of jazz bands over the roofs of extinguished apartment houses at two A.M. It is a booming business city full of marble banks, bronze-fronted elevators, neon advertisements spelling out the names of international millionaires, handsome factories producing canvas shoes, bargain blankets, rayon yarns, chilled meats, surgical dressings, cigarettes, soaps, furniture, glassware, beer. It is a first-class, standard-part, functionally interchangeable city which could be picked up out of the valley of the Plate and set down in the valley of the Po or the valley of the Rhine or the valley of the Seine or the valley of the Hudson with nothing to change but the accents of the hall porters, the incivility of the drivers of automobiles (who are the least civil automobile drivers on earth), the thickness of the knees of the female figures in the public monuments (which are thicker than the knees of the female monuments even in Berlin), and the amount of vermouth in the hotel Martinis.

Such being the city of Buenos Aires it is not at all wonderful that those who look at Argentina with Buenos Aires in the foreground come to the conclusion that Argentina is, or is about to become, a modern, cosmopolitan, highly industrialized nation like all the other modern, industrialized nations of the West. When you are in a city in which the restaurants are like all the cosmopolitan restaurants you have ever seen except that nine o'clock is an early hour to dine and ten-thirty is not a late one; when you are in a city in which the costumes of the women are so much like the costumes of the women in the last copy of *Vogue* that they probably are, and the uniforms of the men are so much like the uniforms of the men on the 5:11 to Port Washington that it doesn't matter whether they are or not; when you are in a city in which the architecture of the new apartment houses is like Passy only newer, and the illuminated waterfalls in the parks are like Rockefeller Center only more illuminated, and the state of the civic improvements is like Rome only more improved — when you are in a city of that international and interurban character it is only natural to suppose that you are also in a country of the same kind. Or at the very least that you are in a country doing its urgent best to *become* a country of that kind. Indeed you may go even further than that. Observing not only the cosmopolitan, world-capitalism of Buenos Aires, but its stir and bustle as well, its new buildings, its well-shod proletariat, its zooming (as of 1937) industrial indexes, its air of prosperity in a world in which prosperity is something to be observed, you may come to believe that you are in the *one* industrial nation on earth which has missed the current industrial diseases: the one industrial nation on earth capable of repeating in the world of the thirties the success story of the United States in the world which ended in 1929.

If you take the second view of Argentina — and most Argentines of the interior together with a considerable proportion of Argentine politicos and not a few Argentine intellectuals take it — you will end up with a totally different conclusion. Argentina of the pampas, Argentina of the enormous plains, Argentina flowing out into the morning beyond the hills like a sea beyond capes as the plane comes down out of Salta into Tucuman, Argentina without towns, with a few roads, with fences straight and wide apart as meridians on a map — this Argentina has as little to do with cosmopolitanism, with industrialization, as any country on the surface of the earth. It is a country of twelve and a half million people of whom a quarter are concentrated in the city of Buenos Aires and its immediate environs and the rest are scattered over an area as big as the United States east of the Mississippi. It is a country in which the distances from house to house are too great for the barking of dogs even on the stillest night, a country in which the cock crows only twice because there is no answer. It is a country so level that even time has no hold upon it and one century is like another; a country so empty that the watchers at night put their eyes along the ground to see the circle of horizon; a country in which the sky is so huge that men plant islands of eucalyptus over their houses to be covered from the blue; a country in which the space is so great that all the visions end in eternity. It is the country of grass, the country without stones, the country peopled with sheep, the country silent under cattle, the country in which the green goes on and on like water, and the gulls follow the plows as sea gulls follow ships — the country in which the women are always together under the dark trees in the evenings, their faces fading into loneliness with the night.

If you believe that Argentina is the Argentina of the pampas with Buenos Aires very small and very far away at the end of the broad-gauge railroad where the stations come every twenty minutes as though the country had been laid out not by geography but by clocks — if you believe that Argentina is the Argentina of the alfalfa fields and the Shorthorn cattle and the ground owls and the jay voices of the parakeets in the fruit trees in the morning, then you will believe that Argentina is not only one of the most beautiful countries of the earth, but also one of the most truly agricultural countries of the earth. And believing that Argentina is a truly agricultural country you will believe that its destiny is agricultural rather than industrial and that its present manufacturing development is of secondary interest. You will believe, that is to say, that Argentina is not a second United States, emerging as the United States emerged from an agricultural adolescence into an industrial maturity, but a very different and very distinct country with a youth and a maturity of its own.

July, 1938.

THE END